SURVIVAL *for* BUSY WOMEN

EMILIE BARNES

HARVEST HOUSE PUBLISHERS
Eugene, Oregon 97402

SURVIVAL FOR BUSY WOMEN
(Expanded Edition)

Copyright © 1993 by Harvest House Publishers
Eugene, Oregon 97402

Library of Congress Cataloging-in-Publication Data

Barnes, Emilie.
    Survival for busy women / Emilie Barnes. —Expanded ed.
        p.   cm.
    ISBN 1-56507-065-8
    1. Home economics.   I. Title.
    TX147.B28   1993   92-41871
    640—dc20   CIP

Printed in the United States of America.

Survival for Busy Women *is dedicated to several people in my life who have contributed to this book and to the many women who have attended my seminars with feelings of desperation, yet with a teachable spirit. These women have shown me how a hassled, frustrated life can become one of hope, with the promise of surviving our busy lifestyles.*

Special thanks to my Bob, who has given so much of his time, love, and writing talents to many of the chapters in this book.

My prayer is that Survival for Busy Women *will be the tool to motivate, encourage, and energize you to begin implementing the workable principles given. May the Lord give you the excitement to work the plan of organization.*

Go for it!

Hugs,

Emilie

Contents

Exhibits
Introduction

Part IV
Survival Through Organized Moving

Part V
Survival Through Organized Vacations and Travel

Part VI
Survival Through Organized Finances

EXHIBITS

INTRODUCTION

One Sunday after church service, my husband, Bob, and I were visiting with some friends. When one woman asked me about my "More Hours in My Day" ministry, I told her about some of the recent seminars I had conducted around the country. All of a sudden, a man who was listening in on our conversation grabbed my arm. "Emilie, we live in a cesspool," he complained. Thankfully, his wife was not within earshot as he told me, "My wife doesn't work. We have three children, two of them in school. Yet she says she doesn't have time to clean the house."

Do you think that's an isolated case? It isn't. In today's hectic society, men and women are so busy that often there is no time left to plan and execute the daily routines of life. So life is lived in a constant panic, trying to stay on top of house, family, and career.

With more women in the work force, there has never been a greater need for basic organizational skills in our homes. Kathy and Bob are a typical couple. Both work, and they have two children in elementary school. But Kathy wants to quit her job. She feels there are too many evenings when she is too tired to cook dinner, provide quality time for the children, do the laundry, and maintain the house.

One night as Kathy discussed her frustrations, Bob insisted that quitting her job was not an option. "If you stop working, how will we make the car payments?" he asked.

"Sell the car," Kathy snapped. "I can't keep this juggling act up any longer. I'm exhausted, and I'm not the woman God intends for me to be."

Kathy is fortunate to recognize her problem before it is too late. She may be able to quit working if her family adjusts their lifestyle. She is also considering part-time employment. However, many women have no choice but to work—it's a matter of survival. And besides, staying at home is no guarantee that you will stay on top of everything, especially if you have young children and are involved in church and/or community activities.

If you can relate to any of these struggles, this book is for you. That's why we've named it *Survival for Busy Women*. This is not some theoretical exercise. Each chapter is designed to give you practical advice to help you organize your home as efficiently as possible. In the process you will save money, feel less pressure, and find more hours in your day to enjoy your family, job, and life in general.

Before we start, I wish to thank the many women who have written and shared so many helpful ideas. Some of your suggestions were incorporated into this book.

Part I

Survival Through an Organized You

Chapter 1

A Thought for the Woman of the Nineties

"By wisdom a house is built, and by understanding it is established; and by knowledge the rooms are filled with all precious and pleasant riches."

PROVERBS 24:3,4 NASB

*T*oday's woman has embraced the 1990s with much excitement. We've come a long way, women. The eighties found us making a lot of changes from home to work, stress, frustration, disorganization, and fatigue. Our priorities went out the window along with our organized homes and meals. We gave up our children to sitters and day-care, meals to fast-food stores, and our spiritual life moved into low gear—not for everyone, but for many. However, new changes are coming into focus. We are tired of the tired eighties. More women are feeling the desire to be at-home mothers and career women. That's exciting. We will begin to see that the working woman will find a balance between work and home and a new interest in home business—85 percent of new businesses are started by women in their homes. It is a personal choice to be at home for many, yet many will continue jobs outside due to need and desire and circumstances.

My mother became a single working parent when my father died. I was 11 years old. She opened a small dress shop, and we lived in the back in a small three-room apartment. Home and career were mixed. Mom not only sold clothing, but also worked late into the night doing alterations. Book work was also done after hours. We survived because we all helped in a time of need and survival. When our children were small, I developed a small business out of our home; the extra money was for extra things. I was able to do that because I felt somewhat organized and in control of our home.

This may very well be the year God will bring into your life the desire to be an at-home woman and develop a from-home business. Yes, to be successful it does take time, creativity, balance, and desire. Our ministry, More Hours in My Day, began out of our home and has stayed there for over nine years. Books have been written, seminars given, and mail orders sent from our door to many of yours.

Our typist, Sheri, has a typing service from her home and is enjoying better profits than ever before. A dear and longtime friend, Rose, has a small business called "Tiffany Touch" where she goes into other people's homes in her area and does anything they need done from organizing a drawer to hanging pictures. A mother with a new baby designed a slip-over-the-head bib that is sold all over the country out of her home. Still another mom created designer baby bottles—she changed baby products into cash of over one million dollars.

Connie Lund, out of Olympia, Washington, created a small devotional flip chart called "Reaching Up to God" and through its sales is sending her daughter through college. When their daughter comes home for vacations, she helps collate and tie. Most at-home businesses develop family oneness as all work together to help one another with a family business.

Direct sales are popular and profitable: Tupperware®, Avon, Shaklee, Amway, Mary Kay, Home Interiors, "Christmas Around the World," Successful Living Books, Choice Books. From home parties to door-to-door sales, these are just a few.

One woman I read about shops for working women, buying groceries, picking up gifts, and running errands from stopping at the dry cleaners to getting stamps at the post office. She even delivered a lunch to a schoolchild who forgot it at home.

Another creative mom does gift wrapping for people in offices. That led to food baskets and then to homemade wreaths and flower arrangements.

Another mom advertised her famous chili recipe for one dollar—and sold enough to buy Christmas presents for the whole family. She was very pleased and surprised. Aimee makes colorful earrings. Women saw them on her and wanted a pair for themselves. From friends to boutique shops, sales multiplied. All kinds of arts and crafts have created many added sources of funds to the family income.

I was visiting some friends who received an adorable loaf of bread, shaped like a teddy bear. This novelty gift is now being shipped all over the state.

Nancy's a single parent who quit her computer job and started her own service in her home. She is able to be home with her three children and still run a very successful business.

Nancy and Elizabeth teamed up and are designing and selling Christian greeting cards, business cards, and Christmas cards, and doing very well.

Some women are working at home as an employee: sales representatives, technical service reps, claim adjusters, and many others who are salaried employees but who spend most of their time in the field. Their employers typically don't provide an office, so their files, desk phones, etc., are in their homes. Many can do part-time employment in the same way. Naturally you have to ask yourself if you have the space in your home for such types of employment.

I have a friend who shows designer clothing from her home four times a year. She sends out invitations with days and hours, then books appointments and helps the women coordinate their wardrobes.

The 1990s woman, I believe, will get back to home shopping and parties from jewelry to clothing to household products.

As we move through the 1990s, set your desires high and chart out your goals for your future this year. Where would you like to be next year at this time? What will you need to accomplish to be there?

When can you start? Possibly now. If your desire is to be working from home by next year, make calls and talk with friends, family, and business associates. Perhaps you need to take a class on business, sales, design, etc.

Many of you may be happy just where you are. Others may want to cut hours to be at home a little more. Whatever you want to accomplish in the 1990s, you can do it with a positive attitude, desire, and creativity wrapped with prayer.

My desire is to see the busy woman get back to traditional values and to use her God-given creativity wherever she may be—in or out of the home.

Changes will come in the nineties as they did in the eighties, but with a positive outcome and with the priorities of God, family, and career.

Many of my readers want to know how to start a home business. Below is a very brief outline of some areas you might consider.

Goals

Actually write down a goal such as: "By February 15, I want to have a Tupperware® business going in my home." With any goal you must also include some action that will be necessary in arriving at your goal. Yours might be:

• I will contact my local Tupperware® manager and see what the requirements are (due by November 15).

• I will enroll in a basic small-business bookkeeping class at our local college (due by September 8).

• I will investigate the equipment needs for a home office (due by September 1).

• I will prepare a budget and begin to purchase my basic equipment (due by September 15).

Legal Preparation

• I will find out from Tupperware® what licenses, permits, and tax requirements are necessary in order to be one of their distributors (due by November 1).

• I will set up a basic set of books that will include inventory, purchases, expenses, and sales listing (due January 7).

Home Preparation

• What area will I use for this new endeavor and how much space will be required (due September 15)?

• Will I need to purchase or build some basic furniture and shelving (due November 15)?

• I will prepare a budget and begin to build or purchase my basic needs (due by November 30).

Resources

• Begin to identify others who are in the Tupperware® business and begin to question them on how they do it (due September 15).

• Begin to attend rallies and training sessions immediately (due September 15).

• Become familiar with catalogs and marketing techniques (due September 15).

• Make a list of future customers which might help me start successfully in my new endeavor (due September 15).

Hours

• Begin to think through how many hours per day, per week, per month I am able and willing to put into my new business (due September 1).

• Will I need to work around husband and children's schedules (due September 1)?

• Will I have regular working hours (due September 1)?

• When will I manage my home with cleaning, food preparation, children's needs, etc. (due September 1)?

Like many situations, it's a lot of trial and error. You'll learn much as you go along, but the benefits will be most rewarding. Be very realistic in your expectations in any new endeavor. It takes at least one year of intense effort, planning, and marketing to begin to see some rewards for your efforts. Hang in there—don't give up!

An excellent resource for you is a new book written by one More Hours in My Day instructor in Scottsdale, Arizona. The title is *The Stay-at-Home Mom* by Donna Otto, published by Harvest House, Eugene, Oregon, 1992.

Trusting His love to touch your life in the 1990s!

Chapter 2

Recipe for Beating Stress

> "A woman who fears the Lord is to be praised. Give her the reward she has earned, and let her works bring her praise at the city gate."
>
> PROVERBS 31:30 NIV

At the start of most of my seminars, I like to play a little game. I ask all of the women to stand up. Then I ask them a series of questions. If they can answer "no" after each question, they remain standing. The first time they answer "yes" they have to sit down. Here are the questions:

1) Did you leave an unmade bed at home?

2) Do you have a messy closet in your home?

3) Do you have a messy handbag?

4) Would you find it difficult to tell me what you're having for dinner five days from now?

5) Do you have dirty dishes sitting in your kitchen sink?

6) Would it take you more than three minutes to find last year's tax return and documents?

7) Did you forget to kiss your husband before you (or he) left home?

8) Do you have one or more piles of paper around your house—on top of the refrigerator, game table, kitchen counter, desk, or on the floor?

By the time I'm done there's rarely even one lady still standing. How did you do? Did you answer "no" to six of the questions? How about four? Two? One? Don't feel bad. We all understand the struggle to control our lives. Don't despair; help is on the way!

It's pretty easy to formulate a recipe for stress. The eight questions just cited are a good start. Here's an even simpler one:

> *3 pounds of Hassles.* Any of life's pressures or traumas will do.
>
> *5 cups of Hustle.* These are common everyday demands and can be supplied by any family member, neighbor, employer, children's club, church duty, or committee responsibility.
>
> *7 tablespoons of Hurrieds.* You can pick them fresh, directly off your schedule, expectations, and responsibilities.
>
> Now stir them up and cook the mixture in the oven of life's trials. Hassled, Hustled, and Hurried—it's a fail-safe formula for a massive serving of stress. Serves one for 24 hours a day, seven days a week, 52 weeks a year. Unless spoiled by organization.

But how can we get organized? It seems like today's woman is putting on a juggling act. Most jugglers can handle two or three balls or objects fairly well. It's when we add one or two or even more balls that juggling becomes interesting.

How many balls is today's woman juggling? She began with herself—her appearance, family, school. Then she added a second ball—her husband. And a third—her home. Then came the children. That's four, five, maybe even more balls. Sounds tough, doesn't it? Now throw in the biggie. The final ball called JOB.

How can we possibly keep all these balls going at once? It seems like they are dropping all around us and we're spending most of our energy picking up the ones we've dropped. And making sure we don't drop the biggie. For if we lose that job, how will we make the house payments, pay the orthodontist, or keep the kids in private school?

For a while, I was one of those fortunate few who seemed to have my life all together. I was happily married with two preschool children and no pressure to have to work. Then one day my sister-in-law abandoned my brother and their three preschool children. Bob and I became guardians of those three children and now I was "juggling" five children under the age of five.

That was 25 years ago, and I survived. I made it because I learned how to organize. I could have caved in under the stress and suffered a chaotic home, a frustrated husband, and undisciplined children. There were times when it seemed like it might all collapse. But I persevered by using time-tested organizational formulas. Today we're the proud parents of wonderful, full-grown children. And the organizational skills I've learned have led to a fruitful ministry and business for my husband and me.

Yes, there is a recipe for beating stress! It's called ORGANIZATION, and I'm glad to share it with one and all:

- 1 quality period of time with God each day
- 1 list of carefully-thought-through long-term and short-term goals
- 1 list of priority activities to direct you toward achieving those goals
- 1 monthly calendar
- 1 weekly schedule book
- 1 pad of daily schedules
- 10–25 (or more, as needed) boxes with lids

- 1 3x5 card file box
- Several packs of 3x5 cards of various colors
- 1 box of file folders
- Several large trash bags
- 1 pad of weekly menu planners
- Assorted jars, shoeboxes, pens, baskets, and trays as needed

Mix the ingredients liberally according to the instructions in this book. Season liberally with prayer.

The result will be an organized home and a happier woman whose "children arise and call her blessed; her husband also, and he praises her." That's the promise of Proverbs 31:28, and you could be the recipient of that blessing!

Are you ready to begin? Then let's not delay a moment longer in working toward a more organized you!

Establishing the Target

*I*f we don't have a target, we can never know if we have hit or missed it. Much time is wasted because we don't know where we're going. If we want to succeed, we must adopt a goal-orientation to life.

Early in our marriage Bob and I felt it was important to set goals. We dreamed of the type of home and family we wanted. We realized that in order to achieve those dreams we needed a plan. That plan became the "Barnes Family Life Goals."

We talked often of those goals, and periodically we adjusted them as our lives changed. The biggest change came as we began to mature in our Christian faith. That's when our goals became more Christ-centered.

Goal-setting works because God is a goal-setter. He's stated His goals for us in the Bible. We're to love each other, obey His commands, take His message to the entire world—we could give many examples. Many of the characters in the Bible were goal-setters. Joseph stored food for seven years in order to feed Egypt during famine. Moses led the Israelites out of Egypt. Jesus came to provide us with the way to eternal life. Paul desired to

23

"know Christ and the power of his resurrection and the fellowship of sharing in his sufferings, becoming like him in his death" (Philippians 3:10 NIV).

No army can win a war without goals. Companies set goals and plan strategy in light of those goals if they want to be profitable. No football team would think of taking the field without a game plan. And so it is with individuals. People who set goals are people who succeed. They are the ones who tax themselves to reach their full potential.They are the ones who find life exciting, who are confident and have a sense of accomplishment.

Goals do not dwell on the past, for good planning can virtually erase the errors of the past. Goals are access lines to the future. They allow us to run the race with the finish line firmly established.

Goal-setting doesn't just happen. We must take time to think long-range in order to effectively plan for the next few days. And our goals must be important enough to work at making them happen. Bob and I have set ten-year goals, and then we've broken those down into smaller goals. Where do we want to be in five years if we're to fulfill our ten-year goals? What about three years? One year? Six months? Three months? One month? Today?

See the progression? How can we plan today if we don't know where we're headed? Sure, we can fill our time with activities; that's easy. But by goal-setting, everything we do is directed toward a purpose that we've set. If my goal for this year is to read ten books, then what book will I read first? If I want to disciple my family, what activities am I going to do? In Exhibit A, you can see how one woman does this. She breaks her goals for the year into three-month portions, sets a target date, and has space to record when the goal is achieved. So she wrote "Read *Loving God* by Chuck Colson" and planned

ONE WOMAN'S
THREE-MONTH GOALS

Objectives	Target Date	Goals Realized
Jan. - Feb.-March Activity Period		
Personal		
1. Read: Loving God by Colson	2/1	1/18
2. Lose 5 pounds	3/1	3/6
Family		
1. Have a short devotion at breakfast	1/1	
2. Be a blessing to each other	1/1	
Career		
1. Enroll in "Elementary Accounting" at Local College	1/6	1/6
2. Apply for new position opening at work	1/15	1/15
Church		
1. Volunteer to be an usher	1/9	1/10

to finish it by February 1. She achieved that goal ahead of schedule, on January 18. In this way, she breaks her long-range goals into small, bite-sized pieces.

One of my long-term personal goals is to mature as a Christian woman. How would that translate into specific goals? Two ten-year goals might be to be prepared to teach and lead a women's Bible study, and to write and publish a book relating to the fulfillment we can have as godly women. Five-year goal activities would be to teach a small group of young married women, to read materials relating to growth for godly women, and to make notes and clip materials relating to the future book. Three-year goal activities include assisting an adult Bible study teacher, attending seminars and workshops that relate to Christian growth among women, and reading materials that relate to this topic. One-year goals might be to attend a teachers' workshop and complete a creative writing class at the local community college. And today's goal activities are to spend time in prayer about my personal growth goals, to sign up for the creative writing class, to sign up for next month's beginner's teaching class at church, and to purchase colored file folders and begin a set of files relating to Christian characteristics that lead to maturity.

In the pages that follow I've listed several goals in areas such as Family, Spiritual, Material, Career, Physical, Recreational, and Financial. If our long-term desire is to become the women God wants us to be, we will be organized in every area of our lives. So for each area I've listed possible goal activities for one, three, five, and ten years, and activities for today in light of those goals.

Take, for example, the goal to raise children who are responsible for their behavior. Ten-year goals could include having teenage children with proper manners, proper respect for authority, and able to carry on an interesting conversation with adults. You can see that in order to reach those ten-year goals, there are specific five-, three-, and one-year goals. And there are specific activities planned for today in light of those goals.

The accomplishment of these smaller bites is what permits us to arrive at our long-range goals. They are road maps for life. They are not cast in concrete. They are flexible and can be ever-changing. However, they help us determine the target. In each of the categories, there are many goals and activities other than the examples stated. However, those listed give a few ideas of how we can begin putting our goals into action.

AREA: *Personal*
GOAL: To mature as a Christian woman

ACTIVITIES FOR REACHING THE GOAL:

Ten-Year Goal Activities
1. To be prepared to teach and lead women's Bible study.
2. To write and publish books relating to women's fulfillment as a godly woman.

Five-Year Goal Activities
1. To teach a small group of young married women.
2. To read materials relating to growth for godly women.
3. To make notes and clip materials relating to my future book.

Three-Year Goal Activities
1. To be an assistant to one of our adult Bible teachers.
2. To attend seminars and workshops relating to Christian growth among women.
3. To read materials relating to growth for godly women.
4. To make notes and clip materials relating to my future book.

One-Year Goal Activities
1. To attend future teachers workshop.
2. To enroll in a creative writing class at the local community college.

3. To begin a set of colored files to compile articles that are cut out as relating to Christian characteristics that lead to maturity.

Today's Goal Activities
1. To sign up for a creative writing class.
2. To sign up for beginner's teaching class at church that begins in October.
3. To go to local stationery store to purchase colored file folders.
4. To spend time in prayer asking God for direction in my long-range goals that relate to my personal growth.

AREA: *Family*
GOAL: To have children responsible for their behavior

ACTIVITIES FOR REACHING THE GOAL:

Ten-Year Goal Activities
1. To have two teenage children with proper manners.
2. To have two teenage children with proper respect for authority.
3. To have two teenage children who can carry on an interesting conversation with adults.

Five-Year Goal Activities
1. To have two children who can exhibit proper manners in meeting people, eating out in restaurants, meal etiquette at home.
2. To have two children who can stand on their own convictions and who are willing to pay the price for their behavior.
3. To have two children who sit in with adults and discuss contemporary topics relating to current events.

Three-Year Goal Activities
1. To attend a training session on how to have proper etiquette in social graces.

2. To encourage the children to share in planning the menus, shopping for the food at the market, and to assist in the preparation of the meals.
3. To encourage the children to be part of the family decision-making process.

One-Year Goal Activities
1. To assist mother with the party invitations. Shop for the proper invitations, assist with party list, apply the postage stamps to the envelopes.
2. To set the table for daily meals; including the center-piece, candles, utensil placement, placemats, napkins, etc.
3. To plan the agenda for our weekly family conference.

Today's Goal Activities
1. To show proper introduction manners when the guests arrive for the potluck.
2. To assist mother in bringing the food to the counter when guests bring their food for our party.
3. To ask the children to be sure to talk with the guests this evening.

AREA: *Spiritual*
GOAL: To learn how to share my faith with others

ACTIVITIES FOR REACHING THE GOAL:

Ten-Year Goal Activities
1. To be able to conduct seminars and workshops dealing with personal evangelism.
2. To publish materials relating to sharing my faith with those in need.
3. To train others in sharing their faith by having a life-style that reflects the love of Christ.

Five-Year Goal Activities
1. To teach a small group of young ladies in the Sunday

school group how to share Christ through their lifestyle.
2. To gather information sharing how others share their faith.
3. To read materials relating to lifestyle evangelism.
4. To make notes and clip materials relating to my future syllabus and speaking engagements.

Three-Year Goal Activities
1. To assist one of the ladies who teaches the evangelism class at church.
2. To attend the InterVarsity workshop at the local university dealing with sharing of one's faith.
3. To read all I can on the topic of witnessing.

One-Year Goal Activities
1. To attend witnessing class at church.
2. To attend Campus Crusade "Four Spiritual Laws" conference.
3. To enroll in creative writing class at local community college.

Today's Goal Activities
1. To invite my neighbor over for a cup of coffee (decaffeinated) and share about those things we have in common, i.e. children, school, husbands, meal planning, etc.
2. To send out invitations for three couples in our neighborhood to next month's potluck in our home.
3. To go to the local Bible bookstore and purchase a new book on the bestseller list.

AREA: *Material*
GOAL: To build a 2500-square-foot, four-bedroom home on one acre of land.

ACTIVITIES FOR REACHING THE GOAL

Ten-Year Goal Activities
1. To move into our dream home.
2. To plant the landscaping with our favorite shrubs and trees.
3. To have a first mortgage of $90,000 with payments of no more than $1,200 per month with a 15-year loan.

Five-Year Goal Activities
1. To purchase our one-acre parcel and begin a five-year payment plan.
2. To begin to identify a reputable architect and contractor in our area.
3. To continue to select and clip from magazines those ideas that we would consider for our home.

Three-Year Goal Activities
1. To talk with couples who have designed and built their own homes.
2. To research the geographic area in which to purchase our one-acre lot.
3. To go to home-builder conventions to see the latest in building materials.

One-Year Goal Activities
1. To meet with the bank to determine a savings plan that will let us meet our financial goals relating to building our own home.
2. To subscribe to two design magazines that preview our style of home.
3. To meet with the total family to discuss our goals for a new home. Also, review the sacrifices that will need to be made over the next few years in order to accomplish our goal.

Today's Goal Activities
1. To make an appointment to meet with the loan officer of our main branch bank.

2. To visit the library and talk to the librarian about her recommendation of the two best architect magazines for our style of living.
3. To sit down and talk with the children about how they can help us with this plan.

AREA: *Professional/Educational*
GOALS: My goals for these are listed under personal and spiritual goals for my life. These will include many of the same activities that relate to these two areas. However, if I want to include additional classes, workshops, and seminars I would certainly want to list them and work toward their accomplishment.

AREA: *Career*
GOAL: To found a small ministry/business to share Christ with women and families through lifestyle evangelism.

ACTIVITIES FOR REACHING THE GOAL:

Ten-Year Goal Activities
1. To speak, write, and publish through "ABC Ministries."
2. For "ABC Ministries" to be recognized in the Christian and secular community as training individuals how to live in peace and harmony with others in their homes, churches, professional lives, and communities.

Five-Year Goal Activities
1. To write and speak at every opportunity related to my topic of interest.
2. To read and clip all materials that will give me a basis from which to speak and write.
3. To interview those I meet who exemplify quality lifestyles, to take notes and journalize for future speeches and writings.

Three-Year Goal Activities
1. To observe those individuals and families which reflect good, wholesome lifestyles.
2. To attend seminars and workshops that deal with my topic of interest.
3. To assist in public speaking at church and civic groups.

One-Year Goal Activities
1. To sign up for Toastmaster's Club.
2. To begin to evaluate my lifestyle to see if someone would want to follow me.
3. To search Scripture to see what is written about lifestyle living.

Today's Goal Activities
1. Call the local Toastmaster's Club and find out how to join one of their groups.
2. Think through and identify one or two individuals who live a quality life that reflects positive Christian examples.
3. Begin reading the Book of John to study Jesus' lifestyle.

AREA: *Physical*
GOAL: To have my weight at 116 pounds

ACTIVITIES FOR REACHING THE GOAL:

Ten-Year Goal Activities
1. To have a well-balanced nutritional diet that maximizes my energies.
2. To maintain a low sodium intake.
3. To minimize the intake of sugar in my diet.

Five-Year Goal Activities
1. To continue to read the nutritional literature dealing with weight control.

2. To continue to listen to speakers who talk on healthful living.
3. To be aware of new research findings on good health.

Three-Year Goal Activities
1. To have a benchmark weight of no more than 112 pounds.
2. To eliminate refined wheat (substitute whole grains) from my family's diet.
3. To be involved in an aerobics class at the YWCA.

One-Year Goal Activities
1. To switch from regular coffee to decaffeinated coffee.
2. To evaluate my consumption of desserts and begin to minimize.
3. To switch from syrups with sugars to raw maple syrup.

Today's Goal Activities
1. To call the YWCA to find out about their aerobics classes.
2. To visit the local health food store and discuss with them current health trends.
3. To subscribe to a good nutritional magazine.

AREA: *Recreational*
GOAL: To be able to take a three-week vacation with the family

ACTIVITIES FOR REACHING THE GOAL:

Ten-Year Goal Activities
1. To enjoy a vacation with the family that utilizes all we've learned over the nine previous years.
2. To use this trip to plan, chart, and estimate the who, what, when, and where of this trip.
3. To use this trip to have the children use their math, science, health, and history skills to plan and execute this trip.

Five-Year Goal Activities
1. To plan a two-week vacation in the Sierra Nevada mountains hiking, camping, and fishing.
2. To assign each of the family members a certain area of responsibility to research, recommend, and plan.
3. To initiate selection of location for the ten-year destination.

Three-Year Goal Activities
1. To plan a one-week vacation at the beach.
2. The family would plan the details of the trip.
3. The children would begin to save part of their allowance for this trip.

One-Year Goal Activities
1. To plan several weekend trips to the ocean, mountains, and desert.
2. The family would plan details for these outings.
3. The children would help plan and shop for the food.

Today's Goal Activities
1. To purchase a qualified camping/vacation magazine that describes various planning aspects for successful vacations.
2. To go to the automobile club to acquire various maps showing details for our mini-vacations.

AREA: *Financial*
GOAL: To be able to build our dream home and to finance our three-week vacation

ACTIVITIES FOR REACHING THE GOAL:
Ten-Year Goal Activities
1. To move into our 2500-square-foot, four-bedroom home on one acre of land with mortgage of $90,000 with no more than $1,200 monthly payment.
2. To enjoy a three-week vacation with the family with no more than $500 being financed for this trip.

Five-year Goal Activities
1. To purchase our one-acre parcel and begin a five-year payment plan.
2. To plan a two-week vacation in the mountains. Emphasis on the finance and budget for this vacation.

Three-Year Goal Activities
1. To research and investigate the various aspects in purchasing, financing, and designing our new home.
2. To plan a one-week vacation trip to the beach; emphasis on how to finance the trip.

One-Year Goal Activities
1. To meet with the bank to determine a savings plan that will let us meet our financial goals relating to building our own home and to our family taking a three-week vacation.
2. To begin to execute a savings plan to meet the two ten-year goals.

Today's Goal Activities
1. See Today's Goal Activities for the Material and Recreational Areas.

How to Set Goals

I find that it is best to set goals with someone, and to put the goals on paper so we can review them periodically. Bob and I have always set family goals together. It also helps to talk with others who know something about our areas of interest. When I was thinking about teaching a seminar called More Hours in My Day, I talked with others who understood the realities of that ministry. Florence and Fred Littauer were particularly helpful. In fact, Florence helped me prepare the seminar.

It's important to set realistic goals, but our perceptions are not always accurate. We need to dig into a subject and adjust our surface observations. We can do that by talking with experts and reading books by noted authorities in our field. The information we gather will help us establish our goals.

It also helps to list the advantages and disadvantages of pursuing a goal. Here are some of the questions I ask:

- What is favorable and unfavorable about this goal?
- What sacrifices will have to be made?
- What are the barriers, and how can I overcome them?
- What are the educational requirements?
- How will it affect my family?

Answers to these questions can help us set short-term goals to help us reach long-term goals. Or we might find that a goal is unsatisfactory because the price—in time, family conflicts, travel, financial risk—is too high. It is particularly important to be sensitive to our family. When goals are set with our husband and children, they are far more likely to support us and contribute energy and resources to help us reach our goals.

Goals are never set in concrete. They can be dropped, amended, even reversed. That's why prayer is an important part of effective goal-setting. Proverbs 16:1,9 states:

> We can make our plans, but the final outcome is in God's hands. . . . We should make plans—counting on God to direct us (TLB).

Prayer helps reduce our pride, improve our thinking, and expand our sights.

It's not easy to be goal-oriented. It takes a lot of hard work and personal sacrifice. However, the alternative is that others will control our lives. When we set our own agenda and devote time, resources, energy, and self-sacrifice to our goals, then we can experience the satisfaction of success.

But what do we do when we have several steps to accomplish in reaching our goals? What do we do first? That's where our priorities come in. . . .

Priorities— What Comes First?

Jean had set her goals and organized her days according to those goals.

But she never was able to complete her daily "To Do" list. "For example, I've got this pile of junk mail on my desk," she complained. "I never have time to go through it, so the pile just gets bigger and bigger."

I asked Jean to show me a typical list of her day's priorities. Here is what she jotted down:

1. Review junk mail
2. Get a haircut
3. Write four letters
4. Make bank deposit
5. Pay bills
6. Attend Bible study at neighbor's home
7. Have lunch with Mary Jane
8. Attend aerobics class
9. Pray 15 minutes as part of prayer chain
10. Clean house (two hours)

11. Purchase paint for weekend project
12. Watch Billy's Little League game at 6:30
13. Prepare chicken dinner for family
14. Solicit door-to-door for United Fund
15. Accept invitation for Saturday's potluck dinner
16. Begin planning for Mary's birthday party

The first thing Jean admitted was that she could not possibly do every one of those activities. She needed to process these options into three categories:

• *Yes:* I will do this.
• *Maybe:* I will do this if there is time.
• *No:* I will not attempt this today.

Notice the last option? We must learn to say "NO!" Too many women assume that their only options are "yes" or "maybe." If we can't say "no" to some things, we become overcommitted and wind up carrying heavy loads of guilt for unfulfilled commitments.

The first time through the list, some of the YES decisions were obvious. Jean needed to make a deposit at the bank, fix dinner for her family, and attend her son's baseball game. Most of the others were not so clear-cut. She didn't see any obvious "no's." She needed a system to help her choose between alternatives.

Making Decisions Using Priorities

Just how does a Christian proceed with decisions where the answer is not obvious? The diagram on the next page can help make such decisions easier.

Priority #1—God: According to Matthew 6:33, our first priority is to seek and know God. This is a lifelong pursuit. When God has first place in our lives, deciding among the other alternatives is easier. We are better able to decide what to read, what to view, how to spend our money, and where to give our time when our thoughts are fixed on what is true, good, and right.

When I feel hassled, hustled, and hurried, it's often because this priority is out of order. Usually I need to adjust my schedule in order to spend time with God. When I allow Him to fill my heart, I relax and have a clearer perspective on the rest of my activities.

Priority #2—Family: In Proverbs we read about the woman who "watches carefully all that goes on throughout her household, and is never lazy. Her children stand and bless her; so does her husband. He praises her with these words: 'There are many fine women in the world, but you are the best of them all!' " (Proverbs 31:27-29 TLB).

How does a woman receive such praise from her family? By providing a home setting full of warmth, love, and respect. Creative moms provide quality time, touching, prayer, and eye contact for each family member. This family seldom questions Mom's commitment to them.

Priority #3—Church-Related Activities: Hebrews 10:25 tells us to be involved in our church, but that is not at the expense of the first two priorities. Actually, when the first two priorities are in order, there is plenty of time to participate in this important area of our lives. But occasionally, there may be weeks where church activities are minimized to allow us to focus on the first two priorities.

Priority #4—All Other Areas: This includes job, athletics, exercise, classes, clubs, and other activities. Some people find it amazing that there is time for any of these items. But there is. God wants us to be balanced people, and that means we need time for work and time for recreation.

You might be asking, "Is there really any time for me?" Yes! It is necessary that you take time for yourself.

You are no good to anyone when you are exhausted, frazzled, hassled, hustled, and hurried. So occasionally you need to do your family a favor and give yourself time to cut some flowers, drink a cup of tea, read a book in a quiet place, take a nap, enjoy a hot bath, paint your nails, visit the beauty shop, or go shopping with a friend. These activities can revitalize you for the activities of home and church.

With these priorities in mind, Jean attacked her list of activities, beginning with the junk mail. "I think I'll just toss the whole pile!" she said. When she was done, her list looked like this:

Jean's Priorities for June 1

Activity	Action-Option
1. Open junk mail	NO—TOSS
2. Get a haircut	YES
3. Write four letters	YES
4. Make bank deposit	YES
5. Pay bills	YES
6. Attend Bible study at neighbor's home	MAYBE
7. Have lunch with Mary Jane	MAYBE
8. Attend aerobics class	MAYBE
9. Pray 15 minutes as part of prayer chain	YES
10. Clean house (two hours)	YES
11. Purchase paint for weekend project	MAYBE
12. Watch Billy's Little League game at 6:30	YES
13. Prepare chicken dinner for family	YES
14. Solicit door-to-door for United Fund	NO

15. Accept invitation for Saturday's
    potluck   NO
16. Begin planning for Mary's birthday
    party   YES

By eliminating three activities and putting four more in the "maybe" category, Jean was immediately more relaxed. I encouraged her to cross off the "Yes" activities as she completed each one to give herself the satisfaction of seeing the list shrink during the day. If time permitted, she could do the "maybe" activities, but if she didn't, some of them might become "yes" activities on another day.

I also encouraged Jean to realize that there may be creative alternatives to some of her activities. For instance, attending a Bible study could be a priority, but she might need to find one that better fits her schedule and family commitments. She might find it to her advantage to fix several meals at once so she wouldn't be in the kitchen for long stretches every day. And there might be some activities that could be delegated to someone else.

Of course, not all decisions can be made so quickly. When evaluating priorities, there are some decisions that may take days or weeks. How does a Christian decide on those priorities when the answer is not obvious? I've made Paul Little's five-point outline from his booklet *Affirming the Will of God* (InterVarsity) my criteria when I face that kind of situation:

> 1) Pray, with an attitude of obedience to God. God's promise to us is, "I will instruct you and teach you in the way you should go; I will counsel you and watch over you" (Psalm 32:8 NIV).
>
> 2) Look for guidance from Scripture. What does the Bible say that might guide me in making the decision? "Be diligent to present yourself approved to God as a workman . . . handling accurately the word of truth" (2 Timothy 2:15 NASB).

3) Obtain information from competent sources in order to gain all the pertinent facts. "A wise man's heart directs him toward the right" (Ecclesiastes 10:2 NASB).

4) Obtain advice from people knowledgeable about the issue. It's best if our counselors are fellow Christians who can pray with and for us. "Iron sharpens iron, so one man sharpens another" (Proverbs 27:17 NASB).

5) Make the decision without second-guessing God. ". . . he who trusts in the Lord will prosper" (Proverbs 28:25 NASB).

Planning of our daily and weekly calendar is much easier once we've established long-range goals. They help us choose which alternatives to say "no" to as we realize that some activities don't fit into our mission plans. What we want to do is minimize the number of *good* things in order to concentrate on doing the *best* things in life.

If you're still not sure about your priorities, I suggest you take a few minutes with a piece of paper and write down everything you did yesterday (if that wasn't a typical day, pick the most recent one that was) and the time you took to do it. Start from the moment you got up in the morning and end with the time you went to bed that night. In addition to that exercise, answer the following questions:

1) How long do you spend in Bible study each day?

2) How much time do you spend in prayer (worship, thanksgiving, intercession)?

3) How long does it take you to put on your makeup?

4) How much time do you spend watching television each week?

5) How much time do you spend in casual conversation on the phone?

6) When was the last time you did something charitable (unrequired giving of time, energy, or substance) for your husband, child(ren), or a friend?

7) Would you be ashamed to have someone see your home as it is at *this* moment? How about on an average day?

8) When was the last time you gave witness to your faith in Christ?

9) (For mothers of preschoolers) When was the last time you took a day for yourself?

Now look over your paper and see how this measures up to God's priorities. Write down one thing you will do *beginning this week* to adjust those priorities.

Establishing priorities is a critical way to beat stress. In fact, it might even save your life. One woman wrote me this note a week after attending my seminar:

> I had an unsuccessful suicide attempt about two months ago. I've struggled lately with a depressed state. But after your seminar I have a new lease on life. I'm motivated and my attitude has greatly improved. Your section on priorities really ministered to me.

The purpose of having priorities is so we won't become overextended. Most of us do a lot of good things. But are they the best? If we know we're always doing the most important activities first, we can relax even when we can't complete everything on our "To Do" lists.

Chapter 5

On Your Way to the Organized You!

"Let all things be done decently and in order."

1 CORINTHIANS 14:40 KJV

fter I finished a seminar on how to organize a household, a young mother rushed forward to tell me, "I loved all the organizational ideas and tips you gave for the family and home. But what about *me*? How do *I* get organized?"

I pulled my Daily Planner out of my purse. This is a tool I have used for years to get me through each day, week, month, and year of my life. I would be lost without it.

Organization really starts with our own personal lives. Once we have organized ourselves, we can move more confidently into the other areas of our lives such as our family, home, or job.

Here are the tools you need to get started:

- A purse-size binder with paper 5½″ x 8½″ or smaller
- Blank tabs that you can label yourself
- A calendar

The following are some of the ways I've labeled my tabs:

Goals

This is where the goals and priorities we've set are put into action. The procedure I've chosen allows me to write down the goal, the date I want to see it achieved, and intermediate steps necessary to reach that goal.

Let's see how Jane has organized her Daily Planner. In Exhibit B on the following page you can see three of Jane's goals for 1992. First is that she wants to revise her will. Note that she wrote the goal on January 2 and the deadline she set for completion was March 1. The first step was to call her lawyer for an appointment, which she did on the second. The second step was the actual appointment itself. There is also a place to write one or more considerations. In this case, Jane was considering the purchase of a new life insurance policy.

Another goal Jane set was to lose five pounds by February 15. The steps were to join an aerobics class, eliminate sugar from her diet, and get a physical exam. Note the column to check off each step as it is completed, so Jane can actually chart her progress.

Jane's third goal was spiritual—to join a women's Bible study. She needed to consider the children's school schedule, and with that in mind she called the church office to find out her options.

Your goals can be in any area, but be careful not to set too many at once. You might want to prioritize them with an "A" for most important, "B," or "C." Areas you might consider for goals are Scripture reading, prayer time, family, household, financial, budget, and career.

Calendar

Purchase a small month-at-a-glance calendar at a stationery store and insert it into your binder. This allows

GOALS

TIME PERIOD	DATE

GOAL: _I will revise my will by March 1st_   **PRIORITY:** _A_

CONSIDER: _New life insurance - dependents_

No.	STEPS	DATE	✔
1	Call for appointment	1/2	✓
2	Appointment at 10:00 for 2/3		

GOAL: _I will lose 5 lbs. by February 15_   **PRIORITY:** _A_

CONSIDER: _Have a physical/checkup by doctor_

No.	STEPS	DATE	✔
1.	Join an Aerobics Class	1/3	✓
2.	Begin Jan 6th	1/3	
3.	Modify my eating habits	1/4	
	A. Eliminate sugar		
4.	Physical exam - Jan. 9th 9:00	1/4	

GOAL: _I will join a Women's Bible Study_   **PRIORITY:** ___

CONSIDER: _Children's School Schedule_

No.	STEPS	DATE	✔
1.	Call Church office for schedule	1/4	✓
2.	Class begins January 14th at 10 A.M.	1/4	

you to quickly view all your commitments. Notice on Exhibit C that Jane wrote down her aerobics commitment at 9:00 A.M. on Mondays, Wednesdays, and Fridays, and her Tuesday morning Bible studies. I put all my appointments, family, and church functions on this page.

Daily Schedule

This section allows us to more fully plan our day. We list our appointments as well as the things we wish to accomplish that day, rated by priority A, B, or C. Exhibit D is Jane's schedule for Monday, May 5. On the monthly calendar, she listed her three main appointments. Those three appointments go on the left-hand side of the page by the appropriate time. She also has scheduled time for devotions at 6:30. Then she's listed various things she needs to do under "Action List." There is a place to check off each item as it is completed.

This tool is useful for the mother who works outside her home as well as the homemaker who wants to get her daily household duties done in a more orderly manner.

To Do, To Buy

This is a place to note all the things we need to do on an errand day. There may be some things we can't schedule on our daily planner. Rather than transferring the same list day after day, put them all in one place. I put down things like:

- Pick up winter coat at the cleaners
- Shop for new pair of shoes
- Stop by the library

CALENDAR

MONTH _May_ _____ YEAR _____

SUNDAY	MONDAY	TUESDAY	WEDNESDAY	THURSDAY	FRIDAY	SATURDAY
						3 Part-I Seminar Orange 9:00-12:00
4 Church Brunch – Bosman's	**5** Hair Cut 10:00 Lunch-Barb P. Car Pool-3:00	**6** Bible Study 10:00-11:30 Carpool-3:00	**7** Car Pool 3:00 Little League Game 6:00	**1**	**2**	**10** Picnic at Beach
11 Church Complin's Brunch	**12** Aerobics Begins 9:00-10:00	**13** Bible Study 10:00-11:30	**14** Aerobics 9:00-10:00	**8** Help at School 8:00-12:00 Car Pool-3:00	**9** Help at School 8:00-12:00 Car Pool-3:00	**17**
18 Church	**19** Aerobics 9:00-10:00	**20** Bible Study 10:00-11:30	**21** Aerobics 9:00-10:00	**15**	**16** Aerobics 9:00-10:00	**24** Garage Clean out
25 Church	**26** Aerobics 9:00-10:00	**27** Bible Study 10:00-11:30	**28** Aerobics 9:00-10:00	**22** Dentist 11:00	**23** Aerobics 9:00-10:00	**31** Garage Sale 8:00-2:00 Family BBQ
				29	**30** Aerobics 9:00-10:00	

EXHIBIT C

DAILY SCHEDULE

MON TUE WED THU FRI SAT SUN	May 5 DATE

TIME	APPOINTMENTS	ACTION LIST TO DO/TO BUY	PRIORITY A B C	✔
6				
7	Devotion Time			
8		Call Women's Chrm.	A	✔
9		Take clothes to cleaners	A	
10	Hair Cut			
11				
NOON	Barbara D. Back-street	Go to Hardware for Husband	B	✔
1				
2				
3	Car Pool	Go by Dairy	A	✔
4				
5				
6				
7		See that Chad does Science	A	✔
8		Hem Blue Dress	B	
9		Read New Book	B	

Notes

This is a place to write down notes from speakers you hear, or to capture important points at meetings, Bible studies, or sudden ideas for a project that pop into your mind at the most surprising times. I use this section to record notes from the sermon every Sunday morning (Exhibit E).

Miscellaneous

This is where I keep topical lists such as:

• Emergency phone numbers
• Dentist/physician
• Babysitters' phone numbers
• Favorite restaurant phone numbers
• Books and music recommended

You may want to label some of these areas separately rather than putting them all under one tab. Two things I include in this section are "Communication Log" (Exhibit F) and "Sources" (Exhibit G). In the first, I keep an ongoing record of communications with key individuals. The example you see is my communications with our insurance agent. The second category allows me to list important sources in various areas. This is a great way for sharing information with friends or quickly looking up addresses and phone numbers without always hauling out the Yellow Pages.

Expenses

This allows us to keep track of our expenditures for the month (Exhibit H). It includes:

SERMON NOTES

DATE: May 4   SPEAKER:
TITLE: Choose For Yourself
TEXT: Joshua 24

Farewell address II —
A review of Israel's History

The pronoun "I" (God) is mentioned
17 x's.

Contrast between Israel & our growth
  A. History   vs. 4-5
  B. Birth of a nation   vs. 6-7
  C. Growth & Adolescence vs. 8-10
  D. Mature Manhood   vs. 11-12
  E. Obedience   vs. 13
  F. Call for a decision vs. 14-15
      (We all serve someone)
  G. Response of the people vs. 16-18
  H. Warning by Joshua vs. 19-24
  I. Joshua makes a covenant
        with the people vs. 25-28
  J. Joshua dies   vs. 29

What is my decision?
Talents?   Faith?   Time?

COMMUNICATION LOG

PERSON/GROUP
Ken Barnes - Blue Shield

COMPANY: Fidelity Insurance   555-4710

ADDRESS: 12345 Willow St. #204

NOTE: Talk to Shirley Simcox

DATE	SUBJECT	✓
1/4	To submit Insurance claims	✓
1/15	Received letter needing Bob's signature-returned same day	✓
2/3	Received check for $205.74 Signed and sent to Hospital	✓
2/15	Need claim forms sent to me. Received 2/18	✓
2/26	ask Shirley to reduce our deductible from $500.00 to $250.00 — Will send rider ASAP - Received 3/14	✓
3/7	Ken called requesting clarification on upcoming physical exam - I wrote letter and mailed 3/9	✓

SOURCES

CATEGORY	
Interior Decorators	

NAME/ADDRESS
Kim Design
17642 E. Jason St.
Riverside, Ca. 92505

TELEPHONE (714) 555-4372

COMMENTS/CONTACT
Does an Excellent job w/Early America.
See: Kim Green

NAME/ADDRESS
New Color Trends
703 E. 5th Way
Newport Beach, Ca. 92660

TELEPHONE (714) 555-4728

COMMENTS/CONTACT
The latest in Paint
& Wall Coverings.   See: Sue Beck

NAME/ADDRESS
The Carpet Mill
24316 Paddock Ln.
Sunnymead, Ca. 92388

TELEPHONE (714) 555-2748

COMMENTS/CONTACT
Good range of colors—
Good installation.   See: Joan Chamley

NAME/ADDRESS
Olson's Furniture
21623 Central Ave.
Riverside, Ca. 92506

TELEPHONE (714) 555-1206

COMMENTS/CONTACT
A great selection of
Period Furniture.   See: Harvey Olson

NAME/ADDRESS
Georianne's Floors & Windows
#23 Flower St.
Pasadena, Ca. 92503

TELEPHONE (213) 555-2306

COMMENTS/CONTACT
A great buy on wooden
2" shutters.   See: Ann Peterson

EXHIBIT G

EXPENSES
ITEMIZED

January				
MONTH/YEAR				

DATE	ITEM	CASH	CHECK	CREDIT CARD	AMOUNT	
1/2	Jim's Shoe Repair	☐	☑	☐	21	02
1/2	School Bus Ticket	☐	☑	☐	15	—
1/4	Market	☑	☐	☐	62	—
1/5	Babysitting	☑	☐	☐	5	75
1/6	Dairy	☐	☑	☐	18	63
1/7	Drycleaners	☑	☐	☐	6	85
1/7	Newspaper	☐	☑	☐	10	—
1/9	Market	☐	☑	☐	50	—
1/10	Allowances	☑	☐	☐	3	—
1/11	Gasoline	☐	☐	☑	18	25
1/12	Car Insurance	☐	☑	☐	123	64
1/14	Dental Bill	☐	☑	☐	50	—
1/15	Market	☐	☑	☐	36	—
1/16	Hallmark Cards	☑	☐	☐	6	05
1/17	City of Riverside	☐	☑	☐	73	26
1/19	Water Bill	☐	☑	☐	29	30
1/20	Haircut	☐	☑	☐	17	—
1/21	Lunch Out	☐	☐	☑	7	43
1/22	Dairy	☑	☐	☐	15	—
1/23	Gasoline	☐	☐	☑	21	13
1/25	Allowances	☑	☐	☐	3	—
1/28	Laundry	☐	☑	☐	14	—
1/29	Pictures	☑	☐	☐	7	24
1/29	Stage Play Tickets	☐	☑	☐	24	—
		☐	☐	☐		
		☐	☐	☐		
		☐	☐	☐		
		☐	☐	☐		
		☐	☐	☐		
		☐	☐	☐		
		☐	☐	☐		
		☐	☐	☐		
		TOTAL			730	57

- Date of expenditure
- Item or service purchased
- Method of payment (cash, check, or credit card)
- Amount spent

If you have expenses related to your work or business, you will want to keep separate pages for home and work.

Prayer Requests

I have seven colored insert tabs for this section, one for each day of the week. On a comprehensive list of prayer requests, I write out the names of friends and family and divide them into five equal lists. One list is assigned to each day of the week, Monday through Friday. I leave Saturday as a swing day for immediate prayer requests. Sunday is open for prayer requests I learn of at church. I also write down scripture from the pastor's sermon that can provide me with scriptural content for my prayers.

On the sample from my prayer section (Exhibit I), you can see how I write down the date I receive a prayer request, the nature of the request, and any scriptural promise I might claim. The far right column is labeled "Update/Answer Date." Recording the results of prayer and dates they were answered allows me to see how God has worked in my life and in the lives of my friends. Of course, not all prayers are immediately answered by "yes" or "no." Some are put on "hold" for a while. But seeing how God has answered the others encourages me to continue praying for the ones on "hold."

While my Daily Planner is a fantastic tool for me as I'm out and on the go, there are some things I need to organize but do not have to carry with me. So at home I keep a larger 8½" x 11" notebook. I have color-coded various pages (Exhibits J through N) for easy reference:

PRAYER REQUESTS

DATE	REQUEST	SCRIPTURE	UPDATE/ANSWER	DATE
1/8	Georgia's mother is sick		Out of Hospital	1/14
1/22	Brad's Escrow		Closed	1/24
1/29	Jennifer's Tooth		Dentist Filled	1/29
1/30	Offering at Church	Phil. 4:19	Met needs	2/5
2/3	Elder's Meeting	I Tim. 3:1-7	Went well	2/4
2/7	Thanks to God for answered Prayer	Mk. 11:24	Everyday an answer	
2/14	Christine's Toilet Training		Going well	3/1
2/21	Craig's loan on his home	Matt 6:8	Approved	3/1
2/28	Mom's Trip to Texas		Great Trip	
3/2	Large Seminar in Northern Cal.	Phil. 4:13	Good Response	3/6
3/4	Aunt Gladys' Funeral		Isn't it good to be a Christian?	3/4
3/6	Inter-Varsity Committee		Good Planning	3/7
3/10	Men's Prayer Breakfast		Four new men	3/10

EXHIBIT 1

• *Home Instructions* (Exhibit J): This is a weekly routine of chores and errands. A quick glance at it each day reminds me to do things like water the plants, set out the trash, and water the lawn.

• *Family Household Expenditures* (Exhibit K): This is a more detailed accounting of our household finances than the one in my Daily Planner. All the bills are recorded here in 20 different categories. This makes it easy to establish and control a household budget.

• *Important Numbers* (Exhibit L): This is a quick alphabetical reference for all important services, from ambulance to veterinarian.

• *Family History* (Exhibit M): Do you have trouble remembering your husband's shirt size? Or the last time you got a tetanus shot? Here we can list each family member with blood type, dates of last doctor and dentist visits, inoculation dates, clothing sizes, and other interests (here's a place to put down gift ideas).

• *Credit Cards* (Exhibit N): List each credit card, card number, company address and phone number, and the expiration date. If you ever lose your purse, you'll be glad you have all this information in one place.

One last idea. It's not always convenient to be opening and closing a notebook. I keep a Daily Reminder pad in my kitchen. There are three columns on this bright yellow paper: "Call," "Do," and "See" (Exhibit O). This eye-catcher helps me accomplish the things I need to do each day, and I can tear it off the pad and take it with me.

Do you feel a little better now? If you just take an hour or two to invest in a Daily Planner, you'll be removing a major cause of stress in your life. You'll be on your way to a more organized you!

HOME INSTRUCTIONS

DAY OF WEEK	ROUTINE CHORES/ERRANDS	SPECIAL APPOINTMENTS
SUNDAY	Christine & Chad's Sunday School Begins 9:45	Grandparents to take home after church
MONDAY	Water front plants Feed bird Bring in paper each morning	Chad's Dentist Appointment 2:30
TUESDAY	Set out trash	
WEDNESDAY	Water front lawn Feed bird	Mail off letters, bills
THURSDAY	gardener comes today	
FRIDAY	Set out trash Feed bird	
SATURDAY	Water indoor plants	

FAMILY HOUSEHOLD EXPENDITURES

MONTH OF *January*

HOUSE PAYMENT/ RENT	FOOD	UTILITIES	FURNITURE/ REPAIRS	CAR/ GAS	INSURANCE	PHONE	CLOTHING	CLOTHING/ HOUSE CLEANING	HAIRCUTS	SCHOOL EXPENSES
929.00	72.13	102.40	Car-76.02	21.00	427.00 Car	72.00	15.00	14.00	25.00	5.00
	50.96			17.50	170.00 Med	23.00	41.00	45.00	7.00	4.00
	34.00			18.00			16.00		4.50	3.75
	83.40			20.00			30.00		5.00	6.04
	24.24									
	62.43									
929.00										
TOTALS 929.00	331.96	102.40	76.02	76.50	597.00	95.00	102.00	59.00	41.50	18.79

DEDUCTIBLE ITEMS

CREDIT CARD CHARGES	INVESTMENTS	MEDICAL/ DENTAL	MEDICINES	BABYSITTING	TAXES	DONATIONS	SAVINGS	OTHER MISC. EXPENSES
47.00 B/A	60.00 Mutual Fund	25.00	18.00	—	225.00	175.00	100.00	60.00 United Way
								10.00 Booster Club
								10.00 Boy Scouts
47.00								
TOTALS	60.00	25.00	18.00		225.00	175.00	100.00	80.00

IMPORTANT NUMBERS

SERVICE PERSON	PHONE NUMBER	SERVICE PERSON	PHONE NUMBER
AMBULANCE	555-4203	NEIGHBOR – Sally	555-0011
APPLIANCE REPAIR	555-4219	NEWSPAPER	555-4738
DENTIST–Merrihew	555-4703	ORTHODONTIST	555-1104
DOCTOR – Turnbull	555-4909	PASTOR	555-0767
ELECTRICIAN – Rusty	555-1001	POISON CONTROL	555-0013
FIRE	555-9996	POLICE	555-5001
GARDENER – Mike	555-4618	POOL SERVICE	—
GAS CO. EMERGENCY	555-5551	PLUMBER	555-0114
GLASS REPAIR		SCHOOL(S) – Elem.	555-9013
HEATING/AIR COND. REPAIR PERSON	555-0013	SCHOOL(S) – Jr. High.	555-1111
HUSBAND'S WORK #	555-0321	VETERINARIAN:	—
INSURANCE (CAR)	555-0112	cat's name:	Tiger
INSURANCE (HOME)	555-0112	dog's name:	Mickie
		ANIMAL CONTROL	555-0014
		SECURITY SYSTEM	555-1163
		TRASH	555-0731
		NEWSPAPER BOY	555-0014

EXHIBIT L

FAMILY HISTORY

FAMILY MEMBER NAME	BIRTH DATE	BLOOD TYPE	DATE OF LAST:				INNOCULATION/ DATE	OTHER
			YEARLY PHYSICAL	DENTAL EXAM	EYE EXAM			
Christine	7/9/83	B	12/83	7/84	—	at 18 mo.	
			12/84	1/85	—	DPT	
			1/85	6/85	—	RUBELLA	
				12/85	12/85	MEASLES	
Chad	11/20/84	B	12/15/85	—	—	6 mo. – DPT	
						POLIO 5/85	

FAMILY MEMBER NAME	SIZES					FAVORITE ACTIVITIES	OTHER CLUBS, INTEREST, ETC.
	DRESS/SUIT	SHOES	PANTS	SOCKS	UNDERWEAR		
Christine		5	2T	Toddler	—	Puzzles,	Bible Stories,
Chad		3	12 mo.	—	—	books, Dories,	singing
Craig	16½	9½ D	32"	9½	32	balloons	
Jenny	7	7½	7	8	Med		

CREDIT CARDS

If lost or stolen, notify company at once.

COMPANY	CARD NUMBER	COMPANY ADDRESS	COMPANY PHONE NUMBER	CARD EXPIRES (DATE)
BANK OF AMERICA		7214 Archibald St. San Francisco, CA 94100	555-8421	
SHELL OIL		1123 Sage Brush Phoenix, AZ 85012	555-3321	
American Express		62431 Hilltop Ln. Boston, MA 02106	555-4306	
Diner's Club		2731 Hale Ave. Los Angeles, CA 90001	555-6626	

DAILY REMINDER

DATE: 5-14

Call:

1. Ben's Plumbing
   555-4221
2. Insurance-Car
   555-4702
3. Lamb School
   Jenny's Teacher
   555-9990
4.
5. Pastor Cook
   555-0233

Do:

1. Take clothes
   to Cleaners
2. Car Pool driver
   this week
3. Take dinner
   to Merrihews
4. Visit Mrs. Jones
   at Hospital
5.

See:

1. That Chad gets
   homework done
2. Hubby for
   lunch
3. Barbara D.
   at ballgame
4. That Christine's
   dress is hemmed
5. Focus on the family
   on T.V. @ 8:00 P.M.

Chapter 6

What to Do with All the Paper

"I, Wisdom, will make the hours of your day more profitable and the years of your life more fruitful."

PROVERBS 9:11 TLB

*M*ost of us can't wait for the mail to arrive each day. We eagerly anticipate a letter from a special relative or friend, or grab for our favorite magazine. At the same time, the thought of processing numerous bills, solicitations, and other mailings can be depressing. What do we save? Where do we put the things hubby needs to read—if and when he gets around to it? And what do we throw away?

Every day we must make decisions about paper— from mail to children's art projects, to church bulletins and notices, to newspapers and magazines—and much, much more. It seems like we must sort through mountains of papers that accumulate from day to day, week to week, month to month. How can we ever conquer this problem and control our paper, rather than allowing it to bury us?

One woman solved her problem by hiring a person to help organize all her accumulated papers. As a school teacher, she had acquired and saved volumes of research, teaching ideas, school notices, and student reports.

Together the pair worked three hours a day, five days a week, for three months during summer vacation—a total of 180 hours each. But the teacher's problem still wasn't solved, because she needed to develop a system for dealing with paper at the moment it arrived.

Sometimes it takes a major crisis to motivate us to attack the paper problem. One lady couldn't use her dining room table without a major paper transfer. That happened only when she entertained company. Another woman's husband, fed up with piles stacked on counters, refrigerator, desk, game table, dressers, and even the floor, threatened, "Either the papers go or I go." That ultimatum caused her to bring her paper epidemic under control.

Paper organization usually isn't a problem early in our single or married life. A few insurance policies, the apartment rental agreement, marriage license, diploma, and checking account statements and canceled checks, lure us into thinking a full-fledged filing system isn't necessary. All the important papers fit comfortably in a shoebox or metal fireproof box that is stored on a closet shelf.

But as the years go by, we collect appliance warranties, instruction booklets, "his" graduate school records, "her" real estate license papers, baby's birth certificate and first picture, not to mention the countless receipts for IRS tax purposes. The result is paper chaos. We dare not throw anything away for fear of accidently tossing something important. We might set up an accordion file or put a few file folders in a drawer in a kitchen desk, but many of the papers are stacked, waiting for that "rainy day" when we'll sort them. When we have to locate an important item, it's a frantic scramble. How we wish we'd gotten organized a long time ago.

Don't despair. Help is on the way. There is one rule and six basic steps for effective paper management.

The rule: *Don't put it down; put it away.*

Most of our frustration with paper can be avoided if we deal with it the first time. Unfortunately, most of us aren't there. So let's see how we can organize so we never have to be buried under the paper mountain again.

1. Schedule time to sort through papers. Put it on your daily schedule. If you don't schedule it, you won't do it.

2. Assemble some materials to help you get organized:

- Metal file cabinet or file boxes
- Plastic trash bags (the 30-gallon size work great)
- File folders (I prefer brightly colored folders, but plain manila will do)
- Plain white #10 envelopes (or larger, if needed)
- Black felt-tip marking pen

3. Begin. Start wherever the clutter annoys you most. Determine to work your way through every pile of paper. Go through drawers and closets where paper has accumulated. Continue at set times until the project is completed. (You may want to make this part of the Total-Mess-to-Total-Rest project we outline in Chapter 8, allotting a minimum of 15 minutes per day for a few days or weeks.)

4. Determine to throw away anything you don't need.

- Perhaps you have a lot of articles, recipes, or children's school papers and art work. *In each category, choose five pieces and toss the rest into your trash bag.*

- Don't get bogged down. Rereading old love letters, recipes, or articles divert you from your purpose of organizing the papers.

- You don't need to keep receipts of clothing you bought several years ago.

• If you're having trouble making decisions, ask a friend to help. She can be objective. Later, you can return the favor when she decides to attack *her* paper piles.

• Keep legal papers and tax records for a minimum of seven years. If you operate a business, you need to keep all papers, sales ledgers, inventory records, canceled checks, and bank statements in case an audit is required.

5. Develop a simple yet thorough file system.

• Label file folders with a felt pen. Files might include:

Bible study notes/outlines	Mortgage
IRS tax information for [year]	Photos/negatives
Bank statements/ canceled checks	Home improvement receipts
Charge accounts	Vacation ideas
Utility receipts	Christmas card lists
Investment records	Home improvement ideas
Insurance policies	
Insurance claims	Restaurants
Car repair receipts	Warranties
Charitable giving records	Instruction booklets

• Label a file folder for each member of the family. These files can be used to keep health records, report cards, notes, drawings, awards, and other special remembrances.

• Within each file, use plain envelopes to separate accounts. For example, in the "Utility Receipts" folder, there might be separate envelopes labeled:

Gas	Electricity
Oil	Water/Sewer
Telephone	Garbage Collection

• When necessary, add files so no one file is too thick. For instance, instead of one insurance file, there might be separate files for house, car, health, and life insurance policies.

• *Handle each piece of paper once.* Decide where to file it, or toss it in the trash bag.

6. Store your files in an out-of-sight, yet easily-accessible place. If you're fortunate to have space in your home for an office, then use a small file cabinet or desk file drawer for current files. The rest can be stored in a closet, garage, or attic. Make sure boxes are clearly marked by number and have a corresponding 3" x 5" card in the storage section of your card file (see Chapter 8 for more details). If a box contains crucial records that might need to be removed in an emergency such as a fire, put a bright red dot on the box so it can be easily recognized.

Staying on Top of Paper

Several women have asked me about buying a home computer to help them get organized. I do not believe a computer will solve the paper problem. The solution is to tackle the mountain of papers as we've described. Then as new paper comes into your home, deal with it right away, filing or tossing each piece. You should have a place to store your bills until they are paid. Once a bill is paid, file the receipt immediately.

Managing the Mail

Now, let's talk about the mail. The key to managing this area of our lives is doing it daily. If it can't be done when it arrives, assign a time sometime that day to process it. One area of your home should be designated for this purpose—a desk, table, a section of the kitchen counter. (However, if you use the kitchen counter, be careful it doesn't become a catchall area. One woman told me she put her mail on top of her refrigerator. It piled so high that it took her three weeks to go through it.)

Remember our rule about paper: *Don't put it down; put it away.* It only takes a minute to sort the mail when it arrives, even if you can't process it at that moment. A simple file system can help you do this. One file could be for letters you want to read. If you have older children, each might have his or her folder to check when arriving home from school. Another file should be for your husband. There needs to be a file for bills, another for things you need to discuss with someone in the family, one for mail that needs to be answered, and perhaps another for those that require a phone call.

Many times people ask me questions by letter. If the person is someone I know, I usually prefer to call rather than write. It's quicker and many times a long-distance call is cheaper for me than writing a letter. (I try to take advantage of the cheapest rates when calling long distance.)

One woman told me she covered shoeboxes with wallpaper, labeled the boxes for various categories of mail, and set them in a row on a shelf. This allowed her to process her mail quickly. Remember, however, that with file folders or boxes, we still must beware of pileups. That's why I believe it's best to finalize action on each piece of mail within 24 hours. This way, mail never becomes a burden.

Here are a few other timesavers for mail processing:

• I consider junk mail a time-waster and toss it. It's tempting to think, "I may use this someday." The truth is that you most likely will not.

• For mail that requires input from another family member, I put a note or question mark on it so we can discuss it. Removable self-stick note pads are great for this.

• Sometimes I don't have time to read publications, missionary letters, and magazines. I slip them into a file folder and take them with me in the car. When I have to wait in a doctor's office or for the children, or even in a long line, I use that time to catch up on my mail reading. As I read, I may make notes on it, and when I'm done I toss it or process it according to its category.

• Address changes should be noted immediately upon receipt, making sure you cross out the old address in your address book to avoid confusion later.

• An R.S.V.P. should be answered as soon as you know your plans. This is a proper courtesy to your host or hostess and he or she will appreciate your promptness. If you can't give a quick "yes" or "no" answer, then let that be known, too.

• Make note on your calendar as soon as an invitation arrives. With our busy lives, we can't depend on our memories.

Mail and paper are a part of our daily lives. We can't make them disappear, but we can manage them. A little organization in this area can relieve a lot of stress.

Chapter 7

Making Time Your Friend

"For everything there is a season, and a time for every matter under heaven."

ECCLESIASTES 3:1 RSV

*O*ver the years I have found certain time-wasters that rob us of the joy of proper organization. At the end of the day we don't have to sit back and say, "I didn't get anything done today." Once we recognize these detractors, we can gain valuable extra minutes and even hours in our day.

Budget Time for Yourself

In all of my books I stress that the readers find time for themselves. It is so important to plan for these activities. You've got to set aside whatever time you need to relax, unwind, and do things that are important to you. Even how you start the day will determine how the rest of the day progresses. You need to start with an inspirational uplift.

Here are some get-away-from-it-all ideas:

• Start each day with a personal time with God. I use this time for inspirational reading of Scripture and/or a devotional book, along with prayer. (Read my chapter on "Prayer Organization" found in my book *Things Happen*

When Women Care, published by Harvest House.) I have found over the years that these few minutes are a favorable block of time. I find that the more I give God the more time I have for other things. The days I include God go better, and the days I put God on the shelf I will most likely have a day with many interruptions and distractions. When the children were young I would get up 30 minutes before the family would rise. Now that they are gone I can get my time with God in a more manageable time before or right after breakfast.

• Hire a dependable babysitter once a week so you can have a regular block of time just to do your things uninterrupted. If you are married, you and your husband need this sitter to allow you to get away for an evening together alone. Periodically, get away for a weekend alone. Often young couples say, "I can't afford that." I come back and say, "You cannot afford not to."

• Make time for a bubble bath by candlelight. What a wonderful slot of time!

• Buy yourself a single-stem rose or a bouquet of flowers. Flowers in the room are very refreshing and have a way of upgrading the spirit of the home.

• Set aside a time of the day for writing correspondence and reading. Fifteen minutes provide stimulation to your system. I always tell women, "Who you will be in the next five years depends upon the books you read, the people you meet, and the decisions you make."

• Schedule an adult education class for one evening a week.

• Enroll in a low-cost exercise or fitness program. If none is available, start walking today. Start gradually and build up your stamina. I use this time now for part of my inspirational time. This is a great block of time for prayer and direct conversation with God.

• Set aside an hour each evening called "Mom's time." The children can use it to do homework, watch TV, or play quietly, but make it clear that *no one* is to disturb you unless it's an emergency. Yes, Dad can have his time right along with your block of time.

• Schedule time periodically with a friend to have a cup of tea or coffee. Use this time to develop close friendships and exchange ideas about cooking, finances, books read, and child raising.

• Enroll in a Bible study through your church.

• Go to a concert with your husband, neighbor, or friend.

• Sit and listen to good, uplifting music. You can do this along with writing and reading. When finished, you will be ready to conquer the world.

Beat the Clock While Dressing

• Begin by reading my chapter "Washing and Caring for Our Clothes" in this book. It will give you a good background.

• The way to save time dressing in the morning is at the beginning of the season when you shop. Buy separates in simple shapes with a minimum of detail and stick to a single color scheme. A good year-round one is tan/gray/cream. Make sure each item you buy goes with three things you already own.

• Purchase a good basic handbag which will go with most of your clothes. This way you won't have to keep switching handbags. A roomy envelope clutch goes with almost anything and can be slipped into a large tote. (See the chapter called "Purse Organization" in *More Hours in My Day*, published by Harvest House.)

• Have a couple of dresses that need few or no accessories.

• Hang clothes by category: blouses, skirts, dresses, etc. Also color-coordinate within each category. Remove your clothes from the dry cleaner's plastic bag whenever possible. Many times you can use the separates to go with another separate, and it will multiply your available coordinates.

• Select your next day's wardrobe the night before and hang it on a special rack or hook. This will save a lot of valuable time in the morning. The decision has already been made.

• Choose fabrics that keep their shape and don't require last-minute pressing: lightweight wools, jerseys, synthetic blends. Since I travel so much, I try to select outfits that I can roll up and put in my suitcase or duffel bag. Rolled-up clothes take less room when traveling.

Select a Place of Your Own

Set up an area for yourself where you can keep all of your lists, calendars, files, menus, stationery, etc. This is your place to work and make schedules. It doesn't have to be a formal desk—just a niche for you. See the chapter in this book called "What to Do with All the Paper" for greater details regarding the paper-shuffling time-waster.

Consolidate and Plan Ahead

• My motto for this year is, "I'm not going to let your poor planning create an emergency for me." Poor planning by yourself or others can truly create stress for me. Plan ahead and reduce stress!

• Group errands together. Shop with a plan. If you're going to the cleaners, check your master list to see what else you can do in that part of town. You may not need to run that errand today. It might wait until tomorrow when you're going in that direction. This time-waster, if corrected, can certainly save you valuable time and money in operating your automobile. My "Call—Do—See" charts are great for helping you group your activities for the day (see Exhibit O).

• Whenever you buy a staple for the pantry, pick up two instead of one. When you start to use the second box of noodles or shaving cream, enter that on your shopping list (see Exhibit Q) and buy two again. This habit will save you needless trips to the market. In our home we all knew if we used the last item from the refrigerator or pantry we were to enter that item on Mom's shopping list. That really helped Mom keep track of what was needed and eliminated a lot of surprises.

• Purchase an assortment of birthday and greeting cards and stock up on all-purpose wrapping paper. (I use white paper all year long. By changing the ribbon it will go with any occasion.) Stock up on note cards, ribbons, and bows too. These types of items can be purchased from Current Inc., The Current Building, Colorado, CO 80941. Write for a free catalog today.

• Prepurchase gifts that are on sale and store them in a special gift box that you have tucked away in your home. When the time comes for a party that needs a gift, you just have to go to your box and it will be there in your own treasure chest. This works great for children's birthday gifts. When the children need a gift for a friend, they go to your box to shop. This is so much cheaper and faster—no time-waster here.

• Keep a list of your family's clothing sizes in your wallet or notebook. When you stumble upon a particularly good buy, you can take advantage of it to save both time and money.

• Keep your family and friends' birthday and Christmas lists in your wallet or notebook. As you run across a gift for Auntie Syd or Aunt Maria, you can purchase it and store it. Cross the name off your list, or you might want to jot down what gift you purchased for that person. It will help when you try to remember what you purchased six months later.

Learn to Use Bites of Time—"Instant Tasks"

In my book *The 15-Minute Organizer* (Harvest House), I attempt to have my reader think in terms of a few minutes rather than a few hours. Few of us have several free hours to clean out the garage, the refrigerator, or a closet. The key is to use the 10- to 15-minute segments you do have to accomplish a small "instant task" that will make a dent in a larger task.

For example, clean one shelf in the refrigerator, clean one shelf in the closet, file your nails, make an appointment to see the dentist. You'll double your efforts if you do these "instant tasks" such as writing a thank-you note while engaged in some other activity like running bath water or waiting for a casserole to heat. My Bob does a wonderful job with this technique. We have a large yard, and he captures valuable time by doing a little at a time in the yard. Don't let those precious minutes get away from you and become time-wasters.

Make a Daily "To Do" List

One of the most basic organizational techniques is writing out tomorrow's "to do" list before you end each day—whether at work or at home. We have a notepad that says "Call—Do—See" stationed at the main telephone in the kitchen. It's so handy to write down that next thought for tomorrow. If you are a procrastinator, it becomes a valuable tool with which you can get started right away. Plus it's so much fun to check off each activity when it's been completed. Some days may be so full you might want to reward yourself for completing your list.

Delegation Is a Must

I tell the women at my seminars, "Don't do anything that you can delegate to another member of the family." This doesn't mean they do all the work and you do nothing, but it means you cannot be "superwoman" and do everything. If you carry the full load, you will very soon become stressed out and won't enjoy your role as a wife and/or mother. Children ages 2–4 can put dirty clothes in the hamper or match socks coming out of the dryer. Our Christine did an excellent job of dusting the furniture when she was four years old. Children ages 4–7 can learn to bathe and dress themselves. At an early age they can learn to set the table and help clear it off when the meal is completed.

Young children ask, "Mommy, let me help," or "What can I do?" Take advantage of their offers. Make work fun and they will come back again. Reward them when they have done a good job. Praise them, praise them, praise them!

One of our mottoes is, "It's not what you expect that counts, but what you inspect." Be sure to go the extra step and inspect. Remember, it won't always be perfect. They are just children.

The Right Tool Saves Time

So often a job is difficult because we don't have the right tool or equipment for the job. With today's technology we can streamline almost any job. Do a time-and-motion study of jobs that take a lot of your valuable time. Is there something on the market that will streamline your task? We live on an acre of property with a lot of trees. During the fall Bob used to spend a great deal of time sweeping and raking leaves. For Christmas two years ago I gave him a gas-powered leaf blower. What a timesaver! Where it used to take two hours to clean up the property, the new blower can do a better job in just 15 minutes.

• Appliances that save time include food processors, slow cookers, microwave ovens, and vacuum cleaners.

• With so many stores having toll-free 800 phone numbers, shop by phone when you can. We purchase most of our clothes and garden supplies from catalogs, and we order at strange times during the night and very early in the morning. The order desks are open 24 hours a day, seven days a week. You don't even have to leave your home to shop. Their selections are varied, prices are competitive, quality is guaranteed, and shipping is speedy.

• The new home computers can be used to organize your home—from an updated Christmas list to a record of your bills and payments. My brother-in-law Ken keeps all of his recipes on his home computer. When we are at his home for dinner and I like one of his dishes, he can print the recipe for me to take home that evening.

Avoid Peak Hour Time-Wasters

• Stay away from scheduling appointments and shopping when other people are out shopping. This is one of the biggest time-wasters. Plan ahead and around these stress hours.

• Avoid banks on Fridays; on the first, fifteenth, and thirtieth of the month; or the day after a holiday. Lunch hours are also a no-no! Early morning or by mail is great for most transactions.

• Carry a "to do" folder with readings, a good book, knitting, note cards, etc. You can accomplish a lot if by accident you get caught in a crowd.

• Be the first on the list for repair people. By midmorning they are usually off schedule.

• Many dentists are in the office by 7:00 A.M. This is a great time to go.

• Try not to drive during rush hour. If you have to, think of a couple of route alternatives in case of a traffic jam.

• Have your prescriptions phoned in to the pharmacy. This will save you 15–30 minutes waiting for them to fill your order.

• Unless it's an emergency, schedule doctor appointments early in the morning or just after lunch.

Make Best Use of Your Inner Clock

Some of us are "morning people" and some are "night people." Study yourself to determine which part of the day is best for your energy level and that gives you the most efficiency. Schedule your most demanding tasks when you are at your best. Since all members of the family are not the same, make allowances for their differences. This knowledge will prevent a lot of misunderstanding and hard feelings.

Four Basic Tools for Organization

Women always ask me how to be more organized and I tell them there are four basic tools a person must have to be efficient in daily activities. The basic tools are:

• A monthly calendar (at-a-glance). At one viewing you can see the days, dates, holidays, etc. I like a larger one so I can write down the major items for the month.

• A daily schedule that has 15-minute blocks of time for scheduling the activities of the day. Remember not to crowd your schedule. You will be frustrated because you won't be able to keep your appointments.

• A telephone/address book. In this you include all the numbers that you need to carry for your daily activities. If in business, you would include those numbers that relate to your business. Your social numbers may or may not be included in this listing. You want to keep it manageable.

• A filing system. Keep it simple! There are many such systems that can be adapted to your particular needs. You might want to read chapter 6, "What to Do with All the Paper."

Time can be your friend if you learn how to make it work as a friend. Many of us waste time because we don't have a clear direction for our life. Have you ever sat down and wrote out your life purpose? It's hard to choose good use of our time if we're not sure what we want to do with it. Successful people do what unsuccessful people aren't willing to do. This has been true in my life and as I have observed other people whom I consider successful. They all know how to use their allotted time as a friend, not as a time-waster.

Start today to eliminate those wasters from your life!

Part II

Survival Through an Organized Home

From Total Mess to Total Rest

*A*re you a pack rat? Before you answer, take this quick quiz. Give yourself one point for every "yes" and zero for every "no."

1. Do you find yourself complaining that you don't have enough room or space?

2. Do you have things piled up in cupboards and closets, or stacked into corners because there is no place to put them?

3. Do you have stacks of unread magazines around the house? (Are you saving them for that special day when...?)

4. Do things often get "lost" in your home?

5. Do you often think, "I'll just put this here for now and put it away later"?

6. Are things collecting on top of your refrigerator, counters, end tables, coffee tables, and bookshelves?

7. Do you have things you have not used for a year, or possibly don't want, lying around the house?

8. Do you ever buy something you already have because

you can't find it or don't want to take the time to search for it?

9. Do you often say, "This might come in handy someday"?

10. Do you have to move things around in your closets or cupboards to find a certain item?

Now total up your score.

        0–3   Looks pretty good

        4–7   Could use some improvement

        8–10 It's never too late, Pack Rat!

If you'll follow through on the suggestions in this chapter, you will be amazed how better organized your home will become. Sound incredible? That's why I quoted Philippians 4:13 at the beginning of this chapter. You *can* do all things *through Christ* who strengthens you. To show you how, we are going to break this huge task into bite-size pieces.

First, decide which area of clutter is bothering you most. The top of the refrigerator? The hall closet? The dresser drawers? That's where you'll begin the process we'll describe in a moment.

Second, set aside a 15-minute time slot to begin to take care of that clutter. Set your oven timer (or a portable hand timer if you are away from the kitchen area) and go to it. You will be surprised what you can accomplish in just 15 minutes. Sure, you won't finish today. But if you take 15 minutes a day for the next few weeks, attacking each area of clutter, you'll soon feel like you're living in a new house. And in the process, we're going to give you a system for keeping your home clutter-free! Plus, you will have a simple plan for keeping on top of the household routine.

The theme of this chapter is "Out of sight, out of mind." We're going to go through your house and throw away or give away anything you don't intend to use in the near future. Our motto is "When in doubt, throw it out."

Now don't panic. We're not going to throw everything away. But everything we do keep is going to be organized so we can find it in a moment. One woman told me that over a five-week period she organized her entire household into 135 cardboard boxes, each numbered and cataloged. "I'm a pack rat," she admitted, "but at least I'm an organized one!"

I believe 15 minutes a day for five weeks can do the job for most women. All of us can find a 15-minute time slot if we really try. That's why I suggest we set the timer each day for the duration of the project. We work like mad for the 15 minutes, then go back to whatever we were doing. Within a week, allowing for one day off, we'll have invested one hour and 30 minutes. Most of us can do a thorough cleaning of one room—including closets, dressers, under the beds—in that amount of time.

Equipment Needed

Are you ready? Let's begin first with the tools we'll need:

- 12–24 boxes (maybe more—remember the woman with 135 boxes), preferably white "perfect boxes"— 16" long by 12" wide by 10" deep, with flip-top lids
- 1 black, felt-tip marking pen
- 1 3" x 5" card file box
- 3" x 5" cards of various colors, and dividers
- Package of 8½" x 11" colored file folders
- 1 file box
- 3 large trash bags (or maybe more, depending on the extent of the clutter)

Now what area of clutter did you identify as bothering you most? That's the room where we want to begin. (However, I suggest you don't start in the kitchen. Save that for the last week because you will need all the experience you can gain from doing the other rooms.)

First take the three trash bags and label them:

THROW AWAY
GIVE AWAY
PUT AWAY

For purposes of illustration, let's begin with the hall closet. Take everything out of that closet. Every item will require a decision and we need to be *ruthless*. If you end up taking a couple of minutes trying to decide on each item, then call on a friend to help. She will help you make decisions you haven't been able to make for years because she is not emotionally involved with your possessions.

After everything is out of the hall closet, return only those items which actually belong in a hall closet— sweaters, coats, umbrellas, boots, football blanket, binoculars, tennis rackets, etc.

What do we do with all the other things that don't belong there? What about those old magazines we have collected for seven years? (That's right—we were going to thumb through them one rainy day and cut out the recipes.) What about those worn-out coats that have hung unused for five years? The baseball caps no one has ever worn? The board games? Old receipts and warranties? They all go in either the "Throw Away," "Give Away," or "Put Away" bag.

Everything that does not belong in the hall closet must go in one of the three bags. Make the decisions quickly. Usually our first impression is the right one.

Once we've completed the hall closet, we move on to the next room. As we systematically go through the house, over the next five weeks we will begin to fill our three bags. If one gets too full, start another.

At the end of the project, take the bag(s) labeled "Throw Away" and set them out for the trash man. They're gone! You'll be amazed how many things are out of the way.

Now we're left with two bags—"Give Away" and "Put Away." The Give Away bag(s) hold things that we might want to give to another family member (baby clothes or maternity clothes that are no longer needed). Or we might donate them to a thrift shop or church rummage sale or a missionary organization. Or perhaps we will want to cooperate with several others who have gone through this same process and have a garage sale. (More on garage sales in a later chapter.) Not only have we cleaned these items out of our house—they have been put to good use.

Storage

That leaves us with the Put Away bag. What do we have in it? Billy's first baby blanket. Some fabric scraps. A shirt our husband wore once to a special party. The possibilities are limitless. How are we going to organize all of this stuff?

It's time to get out those boxes and 3" x 5" cards.

One of the tabs in our 3" x 5" file box will be labeled "STORAGE." With our black felt-tip pen, we number our boxes, beginning with number one. Likewise, we label a 3" x 5" card to correspond to each box—"Box 1," "Box 2," "Box 3," and so on. As we place an item in a box, we write that item on the appropriate 3" x 5" card. We keep going until every item is placed in a box. Then we write on each card where we are storing the box, so we can find it quickly.

When you're done, each box should have a card that looks something like this:

> ## Box 1—Baby Mementos
> —Billy's first baby blanket
> —Chad's baby dedication outfit
> —Baby scrapbooks
> —Billy's favorite rattle
> —Baby's first shoes
> Stored in garage, top shelf

One day our married daughter, Jenny, came by the house with her friend Lynn. "Mom, Lynn and I are making padded photo album covers. I was wondering if we could use some of those remnant fabrics you've stored away?" Jenny asked me.

I went over to my 3" x 5" file box, looked behind the tab labeled "Storage," and found that fabric scraps were in box number 28 which was stored in the garage. We went out to the garage and pulled out the box, and the whole process took only two minutes. Lynn couldn't believe what she'd seen: "If I'd asked my mom for fabric, she would have looked in 10 or 20 boxes and searched through closets all over our house trying to find what I needed." She added, "Mom would have found it eventually, long after I'd found something else instead."

Here are some of the kinds of boxes you might have labeled on your cards:

Box 1	Baby mementos
Box 2	Toys
Box 3	Summer clothes
Box 4	1992 tax information
Box 5	High school yearbooks
Box 6	Scrapbooks
Box 7	Old pictures
Box 8	Snow clothes
Box 9	Scrap fabrics
Box 25A	Christmas decorations—candles, holders

Box 25B   Christmas ornaments
Box 25C   Holiday tablecloths and napkins;
poinsettia napkin rings

That's only a start; you, no doubt, have many more categories for storage. But we're not done. Some of the items in our Put Away bag don't belong in such boxes. We have old newspaper clippings, warranties, instruction booklets, receipts for major purchases, and so on. Now it's time to use our file folders. Here are some of the labels you might want to have on your folders:

1. Report cards
2. Appliance instructions
3. Warranties
4. Decorating ideas
5. Insurance papers and booklets
6. Special notes, letters, and cards
7. Car repair receipts
8. Receipts for major purchases

Some time ago, the icemaker on our refrigerator broke for the second time. When I asked the repairman how much it would cost to fix, he told me, "Sixty-five dollars. However, I believe I repaired it six months ago, so it's under warranty if you can find the receipt." I went right to my file box, looked under "Repair Receipts," and found the required paper within 30 seconds. Then the repairman uttered these wonderful words: "Mrs. Barnes, you just saved yourself 65 bucks!"

Color-coding these files can help us find items even faster: Color is a universal shorthand. Some ways we can color-code our files are:

• By priority: Urgent is red, on hold is yellow, go is green.

- By individual: John is red, Cindy is blue, Christine is yellow.
- By subject: School records file is yellow, financial receipts file is green.
- By status: Active file is red, inactive is blue, canceled or completed is black.

Household Routine

Now that we've got the house totally clean, how are we going to maintain it? Surely we never want to endure such a mess again.

Remember our rule: *"Don't put it down, put it away."* That alone will save stress. Just discipline yourself to handle an item once and put it directly away. If you have a two-story house, you might want to place a colored plastic container at the bottom of the stairs and another at the top of the stairs. Instead of making extra trips up and down the stairs, you can place items in the containers. When one is full, take it either up or down the stairs, sort and put away the contents, and replace the container in its proper location. This is especially helpful when you have young children who scatter toys from one end of the house to the other.

The primary way we maintain our "new" house is through our 3" x 5" card file. Take the dividers and label the tabs as follows:

1. Daily
2. Weekly
3. Monthly
4. Quarterly
5. Twice per year
6. Annual

7. Storage (You should already have this one completed.)

In the first section, we write down all the things we need to do daily. This would include such things as washing the dishes, making the beds, cleaning the bathrooms, and so on. This might seem elementary, yet it's amazing how many women don't make the bed or do other basic chores. It is very important to begin disciplining ourselves to a daily routine and this card(s) can serve as a checklist.

I was speaking at a women's retreat in southern California and a woman came up to me after a session, excited about what she had learned through my books. "They've changed my life," she gushed. When I asked her to give me an example, she said, "I grew up in a home where we *never* made our beds. We just threw three blankets on the mattress and crawled in. So I had to learn and now I'm teaching my family to make their beds. Also, I followed your five-week organizational plan and our house seems better organized and a lot neater. I look every day at my 'daily card' to help remind myself not to forget things like the bed."

Even though the daily cards may seem simplistic, they are important, especially in the beginning, to keep your maintenance program rolling. As you continue to check that card daily, you will establish new habits and soon it will become second nature.

In the "weekly" section of our card file, we write out those things we need to do once per week. We might have seven cards that look like this:

Monday—washing

Tuesday—ironing, water plants

Wednesday—mop floors

Thursday—vacuum, grocery shopping

Friday—change bed linens

Saturday—yard work

Sunday—plan next week's schedule, take a break

Now suppose it's Thursday and Linda, my closest friend, calls to suggest, "Mervyn's is having a big sale today. Let's go shopping and have lunch together." I check my card for Thursday. I can do my grocery shopping this afternoon, but I don't know about the vacuuming. I accept the invitation and the vacuuming doesn't get done.

So what do I do? I can move that activity over to Friday. But Friday is a full day and so I would have to bump something to Saturday. But Saturday I have planned a picnic in the park with the kids. So I move it to Sunday, but that won't work either because we are going to church and we have company coming afterwards.

It seems that if we miss a day, we never catch up. So we break the vicious cycle. If we miss vacuuming on Thursday, that means we don't vacuum until *next* Thursday. In other words, we rotate our cards daily, whether we do the allotted jobs or not.

That may mean crunching on dirty carpet for a week. Some may protest, "I can't possibly do that." But this process disciplines us to keep our priorities in order. Next week if Linda calls again and says, "Let's go to lunch," I can say, "I'll go to lunch if I can get my vacuuming done, because if I don't do it, it means another week before I can do it."

This process allows us to be in control of our home, rather than having our home control us.

The next division is for our monthly activities. We might have cards that say things like this:

Week 1—Clean refrigerator

Week 2—Clean oven

Week 3—Mending

Week 4—Clean and dust baseboards

These are activities we can do any time during the week. Or we might delegate it to one of our children. To make sure it gets done, pull the card and put it on the refrigerator. In this way, every week we are doing a little bit to maintain our home and we don't have to endure a total mess again.

Then there are the quarterly activities. These might include such activities as straightening drawers, vacuuming the sofa and easy chairs, washing windows. Twice-a-year activities might be switching screens and storm windows or rearranging the furniture. Finally, there are activities we only need to do once a year, such as cleaning the basement, attic, or garage; cleaning the curtains and drapes; washing the carpets and walls. These cards are also rotated according to the time of year when they need to be done.

So there you have it—from Total Mess to Total Rest. This is a flexible system that works for any home situation. Women all over the country have found it works, and have found ways to improve it. Susan Wetzel from Austin, Texas, wrote me this letter:

> I prayed that there would be creative ways the Lord would show me to use the storage boxes. . . . Then as I passed by my telephone directories piled near the phone, an idea popped into my head. I stood a box on its "back" so that the lid opens down in front, and stacked the directories, yellow pages, and church directory in it like a bookcase. This way they are within easy reach and out of sight as well.

Susan McMaster from Van Nuys, California, went through the total-mess-to-total-rest process with her fiancé. "It took the two of us every spare minute we could get for three straight weeks, but we did it!" she wrote. "I now know where everything is and in what box, just by taking a few minutes to go through my card file."

Martha McCutcheon in Bellaire, Michigan, put her card file in a repainted kid's lunch box, "So I can carry it from one living environment to another."

Diane from Upland, California, wrote: "I'm on Box 65 and still counting. I've given four huge trash bags full of stuff to the Salvation Army and that was after I cleaned the garage last year and gave them ten bags."

Now let me throw in one more idea.

The Children's File Box

When our children were about 12 years old, I set up a file box for each one of them. (I wish I had started this even earlier.) I gave each child ten folders and one day we went through the total-mess-to-total-rest program in their rooms. After we had organized all of their possessions, they began to file their report cards, special reports, pictures, letters, and other mementos. Jenny saved some love letters she had received. And when she bought her first car, her insurance papers went into the file box.

When the children went away to college, each of them took his or her file box. When they returned home for the summer, their file boxes came home with them. When Jenny and Craig were married, she took her file box, loaded with memories and personal treasures, and began another file box for her new home. Now she keeps all her warranties, instruction booklets, insurance and other papers in one box. So this process can be a great teaching tool for your children.

Now that we have gone from total-mess-to-total-rest, what have we got? More Hours in Our Day! And no guilt feelings about an unorganized house. We have laid an important foundation. From here, let's go on to talk about some of the other stress-producing areas of our lives and see how we can also overcome them. The next area we'll discuss is one of our most time-consuming activities—meal planning.

Chapter 9

Saving Time and Money by Meal Planning

"She is energetic, a hard worker, and watches for bargains. She works far into the night!"

PROVERBS 31:17,18 TLB

*T*he average homemaker plans, shops, chops, pares, cooks, and cleans up for more than 750 meals a year.

Feeding our families is certainly a major part of our lives. For the working woman, it can be a monumental task, especially if we are concerned about the nutritional content of our family's meals. Even the woman who's a full-time wife and mother can find this area an exhausting ordeal.

A few years ago, I found myself often serving as a short-order cook, trying to please everyone in the family. At any one breakfast I might fix French toast, waffles, scrambled eggs, pancakes, bacon, sausage, fruit, cold cereal, and oatmeal. By the time breakfast was over, I was ready to climb back into bed! I had to find a solution before I lost my sanity.

My solution was to plan a week's worth of breakfasts, incorporating each family member's favorite breakfast one morning each week. For example, on Monday I might fix Brad's favorite, French toast; on Tuesday, Bob's favorite, fried eggs over medium; Wednesday, Jenny's favorite, waffles; and so on. I kept Sunday open for the cook's choice, or let my husband cook that morning.

It became such a pleasure to fix breakfast with this plan that I very quickly expanded my planning to all our meals. And it motivated me to begin looking for new and interesting recipes and to scour the newspapers for money-saving sales. Now I always plan my meals an entire week ahead, check my cupboards and pantry to see what I have on hand, and make a marketing list for my trip to the grocery store. It saves me time and money.

As I have shared these ideas with women at More Hours in My Day seminars, they find this system works. Women tell me that they have saved up to $12 per week by preplanning their meals. Hazel Acorn from Jamestown, New York, wrote to tell me that she had taken the idea and adapted a monthly menu plan:

> I planned a month's menu, along with a one-month shopping list. I have photocopied it and have used it for three months now, just shopping once a month. I now am revising my menu selections for the summer months, but I cannot tell you what a freedom this has given me not to have to clutter my mind with the details of shopping and considering what's for dinner.

Menu planning is especially helpful for working women. If it's 4:00 P.M. at work, she can wonder, "Did I take something out of the freezer? Do I have to stop by the store on my way home?" Or she can eliminate that hassle and anticipate going home, knowing she's planned dinner and has all the ingredients ready to go.

This is a flexible plan. If you schedule tuna casserole on Tuesday and find you don't feel like it that night, just switch meals. You have all you need for the alternative. Or if you decide to eat out on "meat-loaf Thursday," simply move meat loaf over to next week. You now have one meal planned for next week and everything you need to prepare it already in the house.

Let's see how the process works. In Exhibit P you can see a weekly menu chart filled out. Let's examine how we can prepare to shop, get the most for our money, prepare the food in the least amount of time, and have fun doing it.

Turning Coupons into Cash

This is a great place to start as we plan our shopping list. Many smart women are saving money by couponing. I have found a 9" x 5½" accordion file is a great tool for organizing coupons. Topics for different sections might include:

- Personal/Health
- Soups
- Frozen
- Poultry/Meats
- Rice
- Baking products
- Baby
- Paper products
- Dry goods
- Breads
- Jams/Jellies
- Cookies
- Charcoal/Lighter
- Miscellaneous

- Mixes
- Laundry
- Sauces
- Cleaners
- Cereals
- Lunch meats
- Soda pop
- Dairy
- Package mixes
- Snacks
- Garden
- Coffee/Tea
- Salad/Seasonings

One important tip when cutting out coupons: Run a yellow highlighter pen over the expiration date. That way your eye will catch the date quickly. Periodically, go

WEEKLY MENUS

DATE _May 5_

DAY OF WEEK	BREAKFAST	LUNCH	DINNER
MONDAY	7 grain cereal	Sack lunch	Mexican Mountains, salsa, dip
TUESDAY	Pancakes w/Turkey Patties		Baked Chicken, Baked Potatoes
WEDNESDAY	Scrambled eggs w/wheat toast		Halibut w/vegetables
THURSDAY	Belgian Waffles w/strawberries		Stir fry w/noodles
FRIDAY	Oatmeal w/rye toast		Italian Pasta Salad
SATURDAY	Eat Out at Coco's	Turkey w/cheese Sandwiches	Bar-B-Q Chicken, beans, biscuits
SUNDAY	Bran Muffins, Melons	Meat Loaf, Potatoes, Gravy	Soup, Salad, Crackers

through your files and discard those coupons which have expired.

Some women save an amazing amount of money with coupons. I met one young mother who said she had saved $850 in one year by couponing. Another working woman saved $1,100. I asked them to share with me some of their ideas that allowed them to save that kind of money. Here are some of their suggestions:

• Use double-discount coupons whenever possible. These are store coupons in the local paper that double the value of any coupon. If your store does not use double coupons, it might be worth driving to another market that does. Used on items that are already on sale, you can save a lot of money. Suppose a store advertises coffee at a special $1.99 price. You have a 50 cents coupon for that brand of coffee. The store also has a double-discount coupon, so you can purchase a can of coffee for only 99 cents.

• Save coupons for "luxury" items (freezer bags, disposable diapers, pie crust mix, etc.) and keep an eye out for these things on a clearance table. They might be slightly damaged or a brand that's being discontinued by the store. With your coupon doubled, you might purchase it at a minimal price, or even for free. I bought a special mix for rye bread, clearance priced at 90 cents; with a 40 cents coupon doubled, the mix only cost me ten cents.

• On costly items, I will drive to another market for a great deal and stock up. For example, since we eat a lot of chicken, I'll look for a sale on chicken, and with my coupons and double coupons, buy up as much as my freezer and budget can handle.

• Couponing allows you to try new brands. You may find a better product in the sampling. But do this wisely. Ask yourself if you would have bought the item if there had been no coupon. And compare prices with competing brands to see if you are really saving money.

• Generic is *not* always the best buy. Often you can get a superior product for the same price or less by using a coupon.

• Never throw away a newspaper before you have clipped the coupons, even if you get more than one food section. Recently my market doubled *all* other markets' coupons, so I made sure to check all the other store advertising sections for their coupons.

• Quickly check all junk mail and clip the coupons before you toss. Also magazines are a great source of coupons.

• Inform friends and relatives if you are looking for particular coupons. They may be willing to pass their unused coupons to you.

• Refunding may be complicated because most markets do not stock refund forms. My rule is that I don't buy these products unless I have the refund form (clipped from a magazine or newspaper). And I try to purchase those items when they are on sale, or with a doubled coupon, or best—both! And it must be something I use often, not a new, untested product. (Who wants three boxes of a terrible-tasting cereal taking up space in the cupboards?) I have found that many refunds are for combinations of foods I do not normally buy or use. And if the refund is for less than one dollar, it's not worth my effort. I find I save more by investing my energies in couponing.

And what do you do with the money you save? One woman told me that she writes her check for the total amount of the purchase before the checkout clerk subtracts her coupons. Then she pockets her savings and uses the money to purchase Christmas presents. Now that's one way to reduce the financial pressure of the holiday season!

Saving Money at the Supermarket

The best way to save money when you go shopping is to plan ahead. Your weekly menu is the crucial element in your planning. Here are some tips to keep in mind when planning your menu and making your shopping list.

Seasonal produce is usually your best buy. Green beans in season cost less per serving than canned or frozen, and provide better nutritional value.

Check your local newspaper ads for sales, especially at the meat counter. Stock up when possible. If tuna is on special, you might buy a dozen cans. They can be stored indefinitely. (More about stocking your pantry in the next chapter.) Eggs stored in their cartons will last four or five weeks. Many markets now specialize in bulk purchases. However, be cautious that you don't buy more than you need; spoilage can eliminate any savings you might have gained. Sharing with a neighbor or relative might make bulk buying more advantageous.

Generic brands are a great way to save money on certain items. Why purchase a top brand of stewed tomatoes when a generic brand will do great in that pot of chili? Generic brand napkins, paper towels, and toilet paper often provide good savings.

Try not to do your grocery shopping on weekends. Most large markets up their prices on weekends, then lower them again on Monday, Tuesday, and Wednesday.

You might like to make a shopping list like the one shown in Exhibit Q. With this list, it only takes a few minutes to prepare my shopping list each week. (Exhibit Q shows a completed list, based on the sample menu.)

Now here are a few tips to keep in mind as you go to the supermarket.

SHOPPING LIST

DATE MAY 5

	Qty.	Cost		Qty.	Cost		Qty.	Cost
STAPLES			**CONDIMENTS**			**PERSONAL ITEMS**		
Cereal	—	—	Catsup	1	—	Body Soap	—	—
Flour	—	—	Honey	—	—	Deodorant	1	—
Jello	—	—	Jelly/Jam	1	—	Fem.	—	—
Mixes	—	—	Mayonnaise	—	—	Protection	—	—
Nuts	—	—	Molasses	—	—	Hair Care	—	—
Stuffing	—	—	Mustard	—	—	Make Up	—	—
Sugar	—	—	Oil	1	—		—	—
SPICES			Peanut Butter	1	—		—	—
Bacon Bits	—	—	Pickles	—	—		—	—
Bak. Powder	—	—	Relish	—	—	**FROZEN FOOD/JUICE**		
Chocolate	—	—	Salad Dressing	1	—	Ice Cream	—	—
Coconut	—	—	Shortening	—	—		—	—
Salt/Pepper	✓	—	Syrup	—	—		—	—
Soda	—	—	Tomato Paste	—	—	Juice	—	—
PASTA			Tomato Sauce	—	—	Orange	✓	—
Inst. Potato	—	—	Vinegar	—	—	Pineapple	✓	—
Mixes	—	—	**PAPER GOODS**				—	—
Pasta	✓	—	Foil	—	—	T.V. Dinners	—	—
Rice	—	—	Napkins	—	—		—	—
Spaghetti	✓	—	Paper Towels	—	—		—	—
DRINKS			Plastic Wrap	1	—	Vegetables	—	—
Apple Cider	✓	—	Tissues	—	—		—	—
Coffee	—	—	Toilet Paper	—	—		—	—
Juice	✓	—	Toothpicks	—	—		—	—
Sparkling	✓	—	Trash Bags	—	—		—	—
Tea	—	—	Waxed Paper	—	—			
CANNED GOODS			Zip Bags			**PASTRY**		
			Small					
Canned Fruit	—	—	Large	1	—	Bread/s	2	—
Strawberry	(1)	—	**HOUSEHOLD**			Buns	—	—
	—	—	Bleach	—	—	Chips	—	—
	—	—	Clothes Soap	—	—	Cookies	—	—
	—	—	Dish Soap	—	—	Crackers	1	—
	—	—	Dishwasher Soap	—	—	Croutons	—	—
Canned Meals	—	—	Fab. Softener	1	—	**MEAT**		
			Furn. Polish	—	—	Beef	—	—
Canned Meat	—	—	Light Bulbs	—	—		—	—
Canned Vegetables	—	—	Pet Food	—	—	Chicken	3	—
	—	—	Vacuum Bags	—	—		—	—
	—	—					—	—
	—	—	**FRESH PRODUCE**			**DAIRY**		
Soups			Fruit Apple	6		Butter	1	—
Chicken	1	—	Oranges	6		Cheese	1 #	—
	—	—	banana	4		Cottage Ch	1/2	—
Tuna	3	—	Vegetables			Eggs	12	—
			celery	1		Milk	1Q	—
			lettuce	1		Sour Cream	—	—

EXHIBIT Q

1. *Avoid impulse buying.* Studies have estimated that nearly 50 percent of all purchases are unplanned. The purpose of having a shopping list is to help minimize impulse purchases that can destroy our budget and cause added stress. There are two times when we are most susceptible to temptation—at the start when our cart is nearly empty, and if we have to double back because we forgot an item on the list.

2. *Complete your shopping within half an hour.* You can do this by arranging your shopping list according to your store's floor plan. Supermarkets are often very comfortable places in which to linger. But that lingering can cause us to purchase items we really don't need. It's also best not to shop at "rush hour." At this time we have a greater tendency to pull items off the shelves without comparing prices.

3. *Shop alone if possible.* Children and husbands can cause us to compromise from our lists. Television advertising can cause kids to pressure us to buy the latest cereal, even though it is loaded with sugar and has little nutritional value.

4. *Never shop when hungry.* Enough said; the psychology is obvious.

5. *Understand supermarket psychology.* For instance, grocery stores stock their highest-priced items at eye level. Lower-priced staples like flour, sugar, and salt are often near the floor, as are bulk quantities of many items. Always check top and bottom shelves for similar items with lower price tags. Also, foods displayed at the end of aisles may appear to be on sale, but often they are not.

6. *Use unit pricing.* Many stores now do this for you. On the shelf tags, along with the price of an item, will be a number telling you the price of that item per pound or per cup. You can compare different brands and different sizes to see which is the best buy. Or purchase a pocket calculator and take it with you to the market to figure

the unit cost yourself. You can also use the calculator to keep a running total of your purchases, to help you stay within budget.

7. *Avoid foods packaged as individual servings.* Extra packaging usually boosts the price. A single family unit or a couple without children might be able to buy this way for convenience. But this is not an economical way to purchase food for families with children.

8. *Compare meat prices.* Notice the difference in the price per pound of boneless chicken breasts compared to whole chicken breasts with ribs. The filets often cost twice as much. You can filet chicken yourself by parboiling for 10 to 12 minutes and peeling the meat off the bone. But cheaper is not always better. Sometimes a relatively high-priced cut of beef with little or no waste may provide more meat for the money than a lower-priced cut with much bone, gristle, or fat. Chicken, turkey, and fish are often bargains for the budget buyer.

9. *Buy produce in season.* Never buy the first crop; prices are sure to go down. Fruits and vegetables purchased at the height of the season are at their peak quality and lowest price. Consider having an old-fashioned canning weekend to take advantage of your favorite produce, so you can enjoy them throughout the year.

10. *Study the labels.* As an informed consumer, you need to be aware of what the labels on your products mean. Manufacturers use additives and preservatives to give color and longer shelf life to their products. You may not be willing to make that trade-off.

What Food Labels Tell You

• *Ingredients.* Ingredients must be listed in descending order of prominence by weight. So the first ingredients listed are the main ingredients in that product.

• *Colors and flavors.* Added colors and flavors do not have to be listed by name. But the use of artificial colors or flavors must be indicated.

• *Serving content.* Information must include the serving size; the number of calories per serving; the amount of protein, carbohydrates, and fat in each serving; the percentage of U.S. recommended daily allowance (U.S. RDA) for protein and seven important vitamins and minerals.

• *Optional information.* Some labels also contain the following: the percentage of U.S. RDA for any of the 12 additional vitamins and minerals, the amount of saturated and unsaturated fat and cholesterol per serving, and the amount of sodium per serving.

What Food Labels Don't Tell you

• *What standardized foods contain.* More than 350 foods, including such common items as enriched white bread and catsup, are classified as "standardized." The FDA has established guidelines for these items and manufacturers are not required to list the ingredients.

• *The amount of sugar in some products.* Sugar and sweeteners come in a variety of forms—white sugar, brown sugar, corn syrup, dextrose, sucrose, maltose, corn sweeteners—and if they're all listed separately, it's nearly impossible to know the actual amount of sugar contained in a labeled product.

• *How "natural" a product is.* FDA guidelines for use of the word "natural" are loose. A "natural" product may, in fact, be highly processed and full of additives.

• *Specific ingredients that may be harmful.* Since coloring or spices that don't have to be listed by name can cause some people nausea, dizziness, or hives, it may be difficult to know exactly which product to avoid.

Saving Time Back at Home

Now that we've planned our menu and purchased our food, let's see what we can do to streamline our food preparation.

One tremendous timesaver is to prepare our food as soon as we bring it home from the market. No, I don't mean cook it—just prepare it. If you already know how you will use your vegetables, they can be cleaned, cut or chopped, placed in plastic bags or Tupperware® containers, and stored in the refrigerator—ready for salads, steamed vegetables, soups, or casseroles. Onions and green peppers can be chopped, placed in an airtight container or plastic bag, and frozen. A large block of cheese can be grated and frozen, allowing you to remove a portion whenever needed.

Salad greens can be cleaned, drained, and stored for the week's salads. An easy way to remove the water from greens is to put them in a lingerie bag (a mesh bag available at grocery and drug stores) and place them in your washing machine on "spin" cycle for about two minutes. That spins out all the water, and the greens will stay fresh and crisp for up to two weeks when stored in a plastic bag or plastic container in the refrigerator. (But don't leave your washing machine while the lettuce is spinning. One woman walked away and forgot about the lettuce and didn't discover it until three days later.)

Fruit prepared ahead of time will keep well if you squeeze lemon juice over it, toss, and refrigerate. The juice of half a lemon is enough for up to two quarts of cut fruit.

Now here are a few other ideas for saving time and money in your food preparation:

1. Turn your no-longer-fresh bread and crackers into crumbs for use in stuffings, casseroles, and meat loaf.

Just put them in the blender, turn it on and count to three, then put the crumbs in a plastic bag for storage.

2. Save oil from deep frying. Strain through cheese-cloth and keep refrigerated.

3. Citrus fruit yields more juice at room temperature.

4. Use the time when you're watching television for jobs like shelling nuts. Children often like to help in this task, especially if they can nibble while they help.

5. Learn to do two things at once when working in the kitchen. I highly recommend a long extension cord for your phone so it can reach every corner of the kitchen. While you're on the phone you can:

- Load or unload the dishwasher
- Clean the refrigerator
- Cook a meal
- Bake a cake
- Mop the floor
- Clean under the kitchen sink

No doubt you can come up with many other ways to do two things at once.

6. Practice this timesaving rule: *Don't put it down, put it away.* We spend many extra minutes handling an item two or three times. Discipline yourself to handle it once and put it directly away.

7. Take advantage of any convenience appliances you have, such as a microwave oven or food processor. They can be a costly luxury if they aren't used; but a wonderful timesaver for the busy mother and working woman.

8. Plan your timetable for meal preparation so the cooked vegetables aren't done ten minutes before the chicken. Vegetables like green beans and broccoli can quickly lose color, texture, flavor, and nutritional value.

Timing your meal preparation may take some trial and error, but with a little practice you will become very capable.

Debbie Thompson of Chino, California, wrote to me after attending one of my seminars. She has more ideas for saving time in the kitchen:

> I decided to try your suggestions of preparing everything I could right when I got home from the grocery store. I started with a few items and then looked at the clock and just kept going and got more and more excited. So I pulled out a piece of paper and wrote down the list. . . . We have never eaten so good for an entire week and my husband is no longer buying lunches out, which saves us more money. Here's what I did:
>
> 1. Boiled eggs for the week
> 2. Made a Jello salad
> 3. Washed, drained, and spun lettuce as you suggested
> 4. Cooked and cut turkey breast for lunches
> 5. Cut carrot and celery sticks, and zucchini, too
> 6. Made a dip
> 7. Packaged nuts and raisins for lunches
> 8. Put all other groceries away
> 9. Mixed the frozen juice for the week.
> 10. Made a potato salad
> 11. Made tuna salad for sandwiches
> 12. Made orange juice popsicles for treats
> 13. Put chips and cookies for lunches in plastic bags
> 14. Made a meat loaf for tonight's dinner
> 15. Washed potatoes to bake for tonight's dinner

I had interruptions and it (still) only took me two hours. Not only did I save time, but money too. Plus it released my stress and frustration over meals and lunches.

Now that's organization! I've prepared a "Saving Time & Money Checklist" (Exhibit R shows one filled out) to help you chart your own progress. All you do is answer "yes" or "no" to each question at the end of a week. If the answer is "yes" to most of the questions, you are on your way to being more efficient and you will have more time and money for other activities. If you answer "no," evaluate how you can change your habit so it can become a "yes" next week. There's also space to add to the checklist. Do this for a few weeks until you can answer "yes" to every question. You'll find meal preparation will become a joy rather than a mental and physical hassle.

Saving Time & Money Checklist

Week Of: _____

OPPORTUNITIES TO SAVE	CHOICE YES	NO	CHANGE OF HABIT
1. Did I plan my menus this week?	✓		*So much easier.*
2. Did I work off a shopping list this week?	✓		*So much faster.*
3. Did I avoid extra trips to the market this week?	✓		*only one trip.*
4. Did I go to the market when I wasn't hungry?	✓		*snacky food was off.*
5. Did I have better timing with food preparation?		✓	*I still need to work on coming together.*
6. Did I take advantage of my microwave this week? My food processor?	✓ ✓		
7. Did I save costs by purchasing seasonal fruits? Vegetables?	✓ ✓		*Fresh Pears. Fresh Corn.*

OPPORTUNITIES TO SAVE	CHOICE		CHANGE OF HABIT
	YES	NO	
8. When shopping, did I do price comparison before selecting an item?	✓		I even switched on a couple of brands.
9. Did I check local newspaper for special ads and coupons?	✓		Saved $4.00 last week.
10. Did I avoid impulse purchases?	✓		No shopping at the cash register.
11. Did I stay within my budget?	✓		I was $8.00 below budget.
12. Did I look for bulk packaging to save?	✓		Beans.
13. Was I able to save money by purchasing day-old bread and rolls?	✓		4 rolls at 1/2 price.
14. Was I able to save money by using more chicken and turkey in my menus?		✓	Not this week, but next week.
15. Did I avoid shopping on the weekend? Busy time of day?	✓ ✓		The traffic jam wasn't there.

OPPORTUNITIES TO SAVE	CHOICE YES	NO	CHANGE OF HABIT
16. Did I purchase a generic brand item this week?	✓		The stewed tomatoes were great.
17. Did I shop out of a catalog this week?	✓		Ordered several items from L.L. Bean
18. Did I reorganize at least one item in my kitchen this week to make it more convenient?	✓		Rearranged spices in A-B-C order.
19. Did I prepare some foods when I came home from the market to save me time later?	✓		Washed lettuce. grated cheese. Chopped nuts.
20. Did I save time in food preparation while watching TV?	✓		Snapped green beans. Cracked nuts.
21. Was I able to apply the rule, "Don't put it down, put it away!" this week?	✓		It reduced the clutter.

OPPORTUNITIES TO SAVE	CHOICE		CHANGE OF HABIT
	YES	NO	
22. Did I eliminate extra steps by pre-planning my activities?	✓		I planned the cleaners, nursery, around marketing.
23. Other _____ _____ _____ _____		✓	

Chapter 10

Planning an Efficient Pantry and Kitchen

"...but gather the wheat into my barn."

MATTHEW 13:30 NASB

*E*very woman should have a pantry. It's an essential element in organizing our meals, saving money, and relieving much of the stress today's women experience. Unfortunately many women do not have a separate room they can devote to a pantry. But you can make a pantry out of one section of the kitchen cupboards. Or put some cupboards in a nearby area such as the laundry room, mud room, or garage. Preferably, your freezer should be located here. And if you have a large family, you might have an extra refrigerator, too. (It can be an old unit, or if you buy a new refrigerator, keep the old one for your pantry.) Your pantry will become a storehouse of confidence right at your fingertips.

If you are starting a pantry, or rethinking your pantry area, use this time to clean off the shelves with a good household cleaning solution. It will give the pantry an extra hygienic smell. You might even buy some cheerful new shelf paper to give the area brightness. Several lazy Susans are great for providing added shelf space and make it easier to reach certain items without knocking over bottles and cans.

I suggest that a pantry contain a supply of basic staple foods, including starches, sweets, condiments, canned or bottled items, and perishable goods. Most of the dry items that have a long shelf life, such as pasta, beans, and rice, can be purchased in bulk when they are on sale. Other items such as perishable foods may have to be replenished on your weekly trip to the grocery store.

Here are some elements that should be in every pantry:

Starches

- Flour
- Cornmeal
- Boxed cereal
- Pasta
- White or brown rice
- Oatmeal
- A variety of potatoes (Red potatoes are especially versatile. They're good boiled, roasted, fried, or in potato salad, and require a minimum of cooking time.)

These items can be used as a staple for any entree, as a side dish, or as a hearty addition to soups and stews.

Sweet-based Staples

- Honey
- Brown and white sugar
- Maple syrup
- Jams and jellies
- Apple juice

Condiments

- Catsup
- Vinegar
- Pickles
- Capers
- Brown and/or yellow mustard
- Oil
- Olives

- Worcestershire sauce   • Salsa
- Canned tuna or any other canned fish or meat. These can be stocked for easy sandwiches, salads, dips, casseroles, and omelets.

Dried or Canned Fruits and Vegetables

- Green beans
- Fruit cocktail
- Raisins
- Variety of soups
- Tomatoes
- Applesauce
- Prunes

Perishable Foods (if you have an extra refrigerator)

- Celery
- Green peppers
- Tomatoes
- Eggs
- Nuts
- Garlic (a great source of flavor
- Onions (green, yellow, and white)
- Lemons
- Cheese (yellow and white)
- Frozen juices

From breakfast to dessert, you will find all of these items welcome helpers in meal preparation.

Here are a few helpful hints for making the most of your pantry:

1. When stocking your pantry, organize your staples and canned goods in categories such as canned fruit, canned vegetables, meats, juices, cereals, etc.

2. Keep an inventory of your pantry (see Exhibit S). Plan your menus using this list and shop only once a week, replenishing staples as necessary. Restock *before* you run out to avoid those "emergency" trips to the market when unexpected company arrives.

3. Leave enough room in your freezer and storage space to take advantage of sales and coupons so you can stock up and save money.

4. Place a colored dot on items you've purchased for a future recipe to warn your husband and children that these are not to be used for snacks.

5. Have a "cooking marathon." This could be fun to do as a family or with a special friend. Prepare several entrees, breads, cakes, cookies, casseroles, spaghetti sauce, or soups. Freeze them in family-size portions (plus a few individual servings), making sure they're labeled and dated. Or try doubling the recipe whenever you cook a favorite soup or casserole. Feed half to the family and the other half to the freezer for later use.

6. Make your own TV dinners by using a sectional paper plate or pie tin and add leftovers to each section. These will provide great dinners after an especially busy day, or when Mom's away.

7. Investigate using a food service. It allows you to save time and money by shopping on the phone and ordering meats and staples for six months at a time. They deliver right to your house, and often put the groceries away for you. This way your weekly shopping is limited to perishables, and often you can zip through the express line at the checkout counter.

Now let's continue to one of the most challenging activities in every woman's home—organizing the kitchen.

Planning the Kitchen

Many women envy a well-planned kitchen, viewing their own as an obstacle course to efficient cooking. No

PANTRY INVENTORY LIST

STORAGE ITEM	QUANTITY ON HAND	NEED TO PURCHASE	COMMENTS
☐ Margarine/Butter	2#	—	
☐ Soup	3 cans	6 cans	assorted
☐ Vinegar	—	/	
☐ Vanilla	/ bottle	—	
☐ Vitamin C	2 bottles	—	
☐ Bouillon Cubes	2 cartons	—	
☐ Chocolate/Carob	/ carton	—	
☐ Canned Milk	/	3	
☐ Pastas			
Lasagna	/	/	
Macaroni	/	/	
Rotelli	/	/	
Spaghetti	/	2	
☐ Salad Dressing	2 bottles		
☐ Cornmeal	3 boxes	—	
☐ Raisins	O K		
☐ Gelatin	/ box		
☐ Pickles/Olives	/ Jar		
☐ Catsup	/ bottle	/ bottle	
☐ Herbs/Spices			
Oregano	—	/	
Thyme	—	/	
Sage	/	—	
Basil	/	—	
☐ Soy Sauce	O K	—	
☐ Worcestershire Sauce	O K	—	
☐ Dried Onion	/ 1/2 bottle	—	
☐ Garlic	O K		
☐ Coffee/Tea	/ #	3 #	Decaffinated
☐ Herb Teas	—	2 boxes	water/process
☐ Wheat Grinder	—	—	investigated-
☐ Other			will purchase
			for June.

STORAGE ITEM	QUANTITY ON HAND	NEED TO PURCHASE	COMMENTS
☐ Basic Cookbook	1	1	Update
☐ Storage Containers			
Baggies	2	2 baggies	
Jars	9		party
Plastic	1	tupperware	Go to neighborhood A
☐ Wheat Flour	8 #	—	
☐ White Flour	2 #	—	
☐ Nonfat Dried Milk	1	1 Box	
☐ Sugar/Honey	OK	—	
☐ Salt/Pepper	OK	—	
☐ Yeast	1	—	
☐ Baking Soda	1½ box	—	
☐ Baking Powder	1 can	1	
☐ Shortening	1	1	
☐ Oil	1	1	
☐ Peanut Butter	1	1	
☐ Canned/Dried Vegetables			
carrot		2 bags	
celery			
☐ Variety of Dried Legumes			
Kidney Beans	2 #	1 #	⎫
Pinto Beans	2 #	1 #	purchase
Navy Beans	1 #	2 #	⎬
Soybeans	1 #	2 #	bulk
Lentils	2 #	1 #	⎭
Peas	3 #	—	
☐ Variety of Grains			
Rice	—	2 #	
Oats	—	2 #	
Rye	—	2 #	
Barley	—	2 #	
☐ Corn	5 cans	—	
☐ Canned/Dried Fruit			
Peaches	—	2 #	dried
Prunes	—	2 #	✓
Raisins	—	2 #	✓
Strawberries	—	3 cartons	frozen
☐ Canned Sauces			
tomato	1	1	
Clam	1	1	
Hollandaise	1	1	
☐ Canned Meats			
tuna	1	3	
chicken	1	3	
Spam	1	—	

matter how large or small, any kitchen can be tailored to suit your style, if you will give some thought to your cooking habits and needs.

Let's start by taking inventory of your kitchen. These are what I consider the essentials:

Pans

- One 10″ skillet with lid
- One 8″ to 10″ omelet pan
- A set of covered casserole dishes
- 1 roasting pan with rack
- 2 bread pans
- 2 cookie sheets
- 1 double boiler
- 1 Dutch oven or similar type of pan

Basic Utensils

Good utensils start with the knives. It took Bob and me 30 years before we finally invested in a good set of knives. Now I wish I'd done it years ago. Included with the set should be a steel sharpener to keep your knives properly maintained.

Other necessary utensils include:

- 1 set of measuring cups
- A variety of wooden spoons
- 1 mallet (for tenderizing less expensive cuts of meat)
- 1 spatula
- Shears (great for cutting parsley, green onions, and meat)

- 1 rolling pin
- Storage bowls
- 1 vegetable cleaner
- 1 cheese slicer
- Tongs
- 1 garlic press (I use this often)

Gadgets

- Grater
- Colander
- Sifter
- Vegetable steamer
- Food grinder
- Egg beater
- Wisk
- Egg slicer

Optional Larger Equipment

These items are long-range money and time-saving investments:

- Mixer
- Toaster oven
- Blender
- Food processor
- Wheat mill
- Microwave oven (A very large gadget!)
- Freezer

The key rule in organizing your kitchen is, "Things that work together are stored together." Take a few minutes to think through your daily work pattern and plan your space accordingly. For example, if you do a lot of baking, set up a baking center. It might be a countertop or a convenient cupboard or even a mobile worktable that can be rolled into your kitchen on baking day. Your mixer, baking pans, utensils, and canisters should all be readily accessible to this center.

Items seldom used, such as a turkey platter, deviled egg dish, roasting pan, seasonal tableware, and picnic gear, should be kept on higher shelves or stored in the garage on a special, easily accessible shelf. That will free space in your kitchen for the regularly used items.

Here are three other ideas for your kitchen:

1. Spices can be found quickly if stored in alphabetical order on a lazy Susan or a wooden spice rack on your wall.

2. Use a crock to store utensils such as wooden spoons, whisks, meat mallet, ladles, and spatula on the stove. This can free up a drawer and allows for quick retrieval.

3. If you get a new set of flatware, keep the old set for parties, to loan out when friends have buffets or church socials, or for family camping trips.

Once you've planned and organized your pantry and kitchen, you'll be amazed how much time you save and how much smoother mealtime preparation goes. Look for new and more efficient ways to store your equipment and food. Study the kitchen and gourmet sections of your department stores for ideas and tools that can save you even more time.

Chapter 11

Washing and Caring for Our Clothes

"Create in me a clean heart, O God."
PSALM 51:10 KJV

*I*t's Monday morning and the kids are madly dashing around, searching for matching socks. A matching pair is nowhere to be found and in frustration you inform your children that the washing machine has actually eaten their footwear.

Sound familiar? Like other areas of home management, our clothing and laundry can be organized in a way that will keep our socks in pairs, save precious time, and in the process teach our children organization techniques.

What about the sock problem? A simple way to solve it is to buy some inexpensive plastic sock sorts or safety pins and pair up your socks before putting them in the washer.

Another time-saver is to have three large bags for dirty clothes:

- A bright calico print bag for coloreds
- A white pillowcase for whites
- A navy denim bag for dark clothes such as jeans

Colored plastic trash cans also make good laundry sorters. Label the cans "colored," "white," and "dark."

The idea is to eliminate the time it takes to sort the clothing; it's already sorted for you. Show your family how to sort their own clothes by putting them in the proper bags or cans. Also announce to the family that whatever goes into the wash inside-out comes out the same way. It's up to them to make sure their clothes are right-side-out.

Now that your family's socks are paired and their clothes are sorted, you can concentrate on scheduling your wash days. Young mothers with one or more children in diapers may need to wash every day. For others, one to three times a week is enough. The important thing is to plan your laundry days ahead of time, and start early in the day. I realize that for working mothers this may not be possible. But leaving laundry for Saturday won't cut it either. What you may need to do is toss a load in the wash as soon as you arrive home from work. If your kids are older, delegate to them the job of transferring the wash to the dryer and sorting and folding the clothes when they're dry.

You might be tempted to start a load right before you leave for work. Resist that temptation. A machine leak or short circuit can cause damage, or worse, start a fire. So never leave the washer or dryer on when no one is home.

Here are a few tips on handling laundry:

• Use cold water whenever possible. This is especially important with colored clothes; cold water helps the colors stay brighter longer.

• Wash full loads rather than small loads. This saves energy plus wear and tear on your machines.

• Remove clothes from the dryer as soon as it stops. If you forget and a load sits for a while, simply throw in a damp towel and turn on the dryer for another ten minutes. The dampness from the towel will freshen the load and remove any set wrinkles.

• Hang as many clothes as possible, especially permanent press garments, on hangers. This will cut down on ironing. I recommend using plastic, colored hangers rather than metal. They prevent marks and creases. Put a few hooks in the laundry area to keep hangers handy, or string an indoor clothesline.

• Colored hangers can also be used to code your family's clothes. Assign each family member a different color and as you pull their clothing out of the dryer, hang them on the appropriate colored hangers.

• Consider color-coding underwear and socks by buying each family member his own color or pattern. If this isn't possible, try marking each person's underwear with embroidery thread or laundry pens.

• Color-coding also works well with folded clothes. Purchase a different colored bin (the size of a dishpan) for each member of the family, and store them on a shelf in your laundry area. As you fold the garments, sort them in the appropriate individual bins. It's up to each family member to empty the bin and put his or her own clothes away.

• Plan one day a week for ironing. (It should be an item in the weekly section of your card file.) One way to help pass the time is to pray for the one whose clothing you are ironing. This can make a normally mundane chore a real blessing and joy.

• Label your linen closet shelves so that whoever puts away the sheets and towels will know the right place for them. This saves time and confusion and keeps your closet looking neat.

It may take a little time and ingenuity to get your laundry organized, but it's worth it. Just think what a relief it will be to see your children going off to school each day with matching socks!

So far, we've concentrated on managing the family's laundry needs. Now let's talk for a moment about our own clothing.

Personal Clothing Care

With the high cost of clothing and fabrics these days, we need to be aware of what we can do to keep our clothing looking fresh and new. Here are 20 ways to stretch the use of your wardrobe through proper care:

1. Dry-clean garments only every eight to ten wearings; less frequently, if possible. Dry cleaning is hard on fabrics.

2. Rotate clothing so that it can regain its shape. A friend of mine rotates her garments by hanging them to the far right of her closet after each wearing. The next day she picks a blouse, pair of pants, or skirt on the left side of the closet. This way she knows how often they are worn. This also works well with the suits in men's closets.

3. As soon as you remove your garments, empty the pockets, shake the garments well, and hang them immediately.

4. Consider Scotchguarding new fabrics. The protection will last until the clothing is cleaned or washed. Then just spray again. Also, use Scotchguard on any of your fabric shoes.

5. Mend rips, loose hems, and loose buttons immediately. My husband has a tendency to tear out the seat of his pants, so I triple-stitch and zigzag the seams when they are new, even before they are

worn. This keeps embarrassing moments to a minimum.

6. Keep from snagging your hose by using hand lotion to soften your hands before putting on nylons.

7. Hang wrinkled clothes in the bathroom while showering. The steam will cause wrinkles to fall out.

8. Let perfumes and deodorants dry on your body before dressing to prevent garment damage.

9. I put a scarf over my head before pulling on a garment to prevent a messed hairdo and makeup smudges and stains.

10. Hang blazers and coats on padded hangers to avoid hanger marks.

11. Store sweaters in a drawer or shelf rather than on a hanger to prevent stretching.

12. Skirts and pants are best hung on hangers with clips—or you can use clothespins on wire hangers.

13. Even good jewelry can discolor your clothing, so dab the back of it with clear nail polish. The polish can also be painted on jewelry with rough edges that may pull fibers of fabrics. (You probably shouldn't do this with real gold or silver as it will ruin the value of the jewelry.)

14. Some stick pins can run or make holes in delicate fabrics. Don't wear them if you are in doubt.

15. Be sure to keep your good leather shoes polished to retain shine and help preserve the leather.

16. Brush suede shoes with a suede brush that brings up the nap. You can use a nail file to rub off any little spots.

17. Replace heels and soles on your shoes before they wear down and cause damage.

18. If your shoes get wet, stuff them with paper towels or newspaper and allow them to dry away from heat.

19. Shoe trees are a great way to keep the shape in your shoes.

20. When storing leather handbags or shoes, never put them in plastic bags. That can cause the leather to dry out. Use fabric shoebags or wrap shoes in tissue and put them in shoeboxes.

And now a word about planning and maintaining your wardrobe. This is an important element for enhancing your professional and personal image. Remember, you rarely get a second chance to make a first impression. These three P's summarize my philosophy:

- Plan—your wardrobe
- Prepare—your look
- Present—yourself

Clean out your closet: Remove everything you don't wear, don't like, or don't feel good about wearing.

Inventory your clothes: Take a wardrobe inventory (see Exhibit T). As you review your inventory list, you can quickly see your overages (those clothes that are old and out-of-style) and shortages. Your overages are candidates for a future garage sale. Your shortage list helps you plan your shopping. With today's buying alternatives, you can find a wide range of quality and price in clothing. I prefer to purchase quality garments that will last longer, in order to maximize my dollar value.

Plan a wardrobe that works: Start with three basic items in a solid color and the same fabric: a blazer or jacket, a skirt, and pants. Then add blouses in solid or print

WARDROBE INVENTORY

BLOUSES	PANTS	SKIRTS

JACKETS	SWEATERS	DRESSES

GOWNS	LINGERIE	SHOES

JEWELRY

THINGS I NEVER WEAR	THINGS I NEED

colors to coordinate, and a couple of sweaters and accessories such as scarves, ribbon ties, belts, jewelry, and a silk flower or two. Select each item so it can mix and match with the three basic clothing items. For shoes, choose one casual pair and one dressy pair to complement your basics. With a little imagination and these six to nine items, you can create 20 outfits!

Each season, or whenever possible, add one new basic outfit to your wardrobe. If you have a trained professional color and wardrobe consultant in your area, you might want to consider investing in that service. It will save you time in shopping and you'll know that you're selecting the color and clothing style that makes you look your best.

Closet Smarts

A well-kept wardrobe makes the best impression to yourself and to others. Keep your clothes in shape the easy way with these closet tips:

• To eliminate wrinkles and creases, hang up a suit or dress immediately after wearing. Since the material retains body heat, the wrinkles fall out more easily.

• For longer wear and better fit, cashmere and wool clothing should be briskly shaken after each wearing, and then hung to air out before being put away in a closet.

• To prevent a horizontal trouser crease midway up the trouser leg, put unprinted newsprint over a hanger rod, then fold the trousers over that. You may also want to purchase the type of hangers which clasp on the trouser cuffs and hang the trousers vertically from your clothes pole.

• Hang your clothes on wooden or plastic hangers, being sure to close zippers and buttons. Make sure that shoulders, sleeves, and creases are straight and collars lay flat.

• You can de-wrinkle clothing in a hurry by running hot water in the bathtub or shower and hanging clothes on a rod. The steam will remove the wrinkles very quickly.

• Overloading clothes in the dryer not only causes wrinkling but reduces heat efficiency and prolongs drying time.

• Slip rubber bands on the ends of wire hangers to keep clothes from falling to the closet floor.

• Wind cellophane tape around wire hangers to prevent them from leaving rust stains on clothing.

• Double the strength of wire hangers by taping two together with adhesive or cellophane tape.

• When storing a hanging garment in a plastic bag from the cleaners, use a twist tie to seal any openings against dust.

Storage

• Moths love grease spots as much as they love wool. Dry-clean or launder woolen articles before storing.

• Moth preventatives should be hung as high as possible in the closet because the fumes filter downward.

• To store sweaters, fold them in your dresser drawer. Hangers distort the shoulder shape of a sweater and stretch the garment unnecessarily. If you can afford the special sweater bags, use them; the sweater looks great and wears much longer.

• To reduce wrinkles, lay a panel of tissue paper over the back of a garment before folding it.

• Heavily embroidered or sequined clothing should be stored flat. Hanging these garments will destroy their shape.

Change in a Hurry

• Keep one foolproof outfit, complete with belt and scarf, up front in your closet. It's a lifesaver for rushed mornings, or when you have to get dressed in an emergency.

• Don't waste time rummaging through shoe-boxes to find that special pair of shoes. Instead, cut one end off each box, then stack the boxes on a shelf beside or on top of each other. You'll be able to select at a glance. Another quick-finder idea is to cover your boxes with wallpaper to match your room or matching adhesive contact paper and staple a 3" x 5" card describing the contents to the end of the box. Color will liven up your day.

A way to make several sweet-smelling sachets is to melt one-half cup of paraffin in a double boiler over low heat. (Keep children away from the stove; the wax becomes very hot.) Remove from the heat, let cool slightly, and then stir in six drops of lavender or other perfumed oil. Lightly coat with petroleum jelly the inner surfaces of the caps from small jars. Pour the liquid mixture into the jar-cap molds and let it cool and solidify overnight. In the morning tap the cooled cakes out of their molds. You might want to get really fancy and wrap them in small pieces of netting with lace trim.

Shoe Sense

Shoes and stockings take a beating through everyday wear, but you can make them last longer with some timely tips.

• Change shoes daily to double their life. Airing them out between wearings prevents perspiration from rotting the leather.

• Consider buying your summer shoes a half-size larger for extra room; your feet swell in the heat.

• Invest in shoes that are neutral in color such as peanut, butterscotch, or caramel. These colors will complement most colors of clothing. Oh yes, you can get "radical" and have a few wild colors for those special outfits.

• Avoid wearing either very flat or very high-heeled shoes. Neither style is designed to provide good arch support for your feet.

• When buying shoes you'll be wearing a lot, choose a pair made of leather, canvas, or woven fabric. Since these materials breathe, the shoes will be much more comfortable to wear than synthetics.

• Roughen up the bottom of the soles of your new shoes so you won't slip. Sandpaper works well.

• Insert shoe trees immediately after removing shoes since they're still warm and pliable.

• Never store leather shoes in plastic bags. The plastic keeps the leather from breathing.

• Shake baking soda into shoes to help banish perspiration odors.

• Keep your shoes well-polished to provide beauty as well as to prolong their life span.

• Remove water stains on leather shoes by rubbing them with a cloth dipped in a vinegar/water solution.

• Lemon juice is an excellent polish for black or tan leather shoes. Follow by buffing with a soft cloth.

• Scuff marks on white or pastel shoes can be removed by rubbing the spot with nail polish remover.

• Patent leather shoes can be made to look like new with a dab of petroleum jelly. It also prevents them from cracking in the winter.

• You can rub dirt off suede shoes with an artist's gum eraser, then buff with sandpaper.

Stocking Sense

• Buy two or three identical pairs of pantyhose. If you get a snag or run in one leg, you can cut it off and match it with a second pair which also has one good leg.

• Your pantyhose will last longer if you give them the following treatment before the first wearing: Immerse the hose in water, wring them out, put them in a plastic bag, and place the bag in the freezer. Once frozen, remove the pantyhose from the freezer and hang them up to dry. It really works.

• A proper fit in pantyhose is essential for long, comfortable wear. A size too small will run easily because of no elasticity; a size too big or too long will wrinkle and bag at the knees.

• Wear a pair of thin white cotton or rubber gloves while putting on or removing your hose to reduce the chance of snagging the stockings with your fingernails.

• If a stocking runs, repair it with colorless nail polish or hairspray.

• If you have mismatched stockings left over from various pairs, you can dye them all the same color by boiling them in water along with two tea bags. Let them sit in the water until it cools, and then rinse and dry your newly matched hose.

• Save fine nylons from snagging in your dresser drawer by placing them in plastic bags. Roll up the bags and slip them inside cardboard toilet paper rolls or paper towel rolls (the size would depend on the space in your drawer). These rolls can be neatly arranged and the contents written on the outside for easy identification.

• Dab a bright shade of nail polish on the tag or waistband of pantyhose suitable only for wearing under slacks because of runs or snags. This simplifies finding the right pair early in the morning.

Cleaning and Organizing the Garage

*H*elp! Come fast! Here, in the garage! I'm buried under the newspapers and magazines."

Ever felt like that? Maybe you've actually had a pile of clutter collapse around you in the garage ... or lived in fear of such an occurrence. That's when you know you can no longer postpone the big event. You really must clean the garage.

Where do we begin in this awesome task? Well, the first thing you need to do is set a date and time. Call a family meeting and ask the family to help "poor Mom" clean the garage. Agree on the date—say next Saturday at 9:00 A.M.—and mark it clearly on your calendar. No absences are excused!

Then as the big day draws closer, assemble the following items:

- Trash bags.
- Jars-mayonnaise, peanut butter, and jelly size.
- Small metal cabinets with plastic drawers. You can purchase these at a hardware store. These can take the place of the jars.

- Large hooks—the type on which you can hang bicycles.
- Boxes—cardboard-type used for apples and oranges. Most supermarkets have them. (Many stores tear the boxes apart as soon as they are emptied. You may want to ask ahead to see if the produce manager can save a few for you.) "Perfect boxes" are great for storage and display of materials.
- Broom and rake hooks. These can also be purchased at hardware stores.
- One to four plastic trash cans—for uses *other* than trash.
- Two to six empty coffee cans.
- Black marking pen.
- Three plastic trash bags marked "Put Away," "Throw Away," and "Give Away."

That's right! We're moving from Total Mess to Total Rest. The principles are similar for every area of our home. We're attacking the garage separately because it often escapes the scrutiny of the rest of our house. Surely organizing this space can relieve some more of our stress.

There's a little more preparation you need to do for the big day. First, make a list of all the jobs required. Then delegate responsibilities to each member of the family. Or, these responsibilities can be written on pieces of paper and placed in a basket. On the big day, have each family member (plus friends and neighbors—recruit as much help as you want and make it a party!) draw one or more jobs from the basket. Keep going around until all the jobs are assigned. Here's an example:

Jenny: Sort all nails, screws, nuts, and washers into different jars or in the metal organizational cabinet you purchased.

Brad: Separate tools—hammers, wrenches, screwdrivers, etc. Put them into the empty coffee cans you have prelabeled with the black marking pen.

Dad: Sort your possessions—papers, pipes, power tools, etc.—and place them in jars and cardboard boxes. Label containers with the black marking pen.

Craig: Neatly roll up the hoses, extension cords, wires, ropes, and any other roll-up type of material. Put all gardening tools with long handles—rake, shovel, edger, broom—into one of the trash cans, or hang these tools on a wall in the garage, using the specially-purchased hooks.

Micky: Empty the large bag of dried dog food into another of the plastic trash cans and cover with a tight lid. This will keep the food fresh and prevent mice and other little animals from enjoying it.

Mark: Collect all the rags, old towels, and sheets and fold neatly into a trash can or a cardboard box. Mark the container accordingly. Make sure none of the rags are saturated with a flammable substance (they should be tossed). This job should be done away from the flame of a water heater or furnace.

Mom: Arrange and label the cardboard boxes and store them on shelves. You might want to organize according to priority. For example, you don't need the Christmas ornaments on a lower shelf since they're used only once a year. (See Chapter 8 for more details.)

Everyone can help fill the "Put Away," "Throw Away," and "Give Away" trash bags. You might want to designate yourself as the final arbitration in case of indecision. But make sure the bags are used. You'll find old newspapers, magazines, empty or dried-up cans of paint. These things should be thrown away.

Bicycles can be hung on the rafters with the large hooks you purchased at the hardware store. Most cars can park easily under them in the average garage. If some of the bicycles are used every day, then maybe Dad or an older son can make a bike rack.

Partially-used bags of cement, fertilizer, and other dry materials can be stored in the plastic trash cans with lids. This will keep the materials dry.

Items such as gardening pots, bricks, and flats can be neatly stored on a shelf or outside the garage. You might build a few outside shelves for that purpose. Winter weather won't harm them, and you have little need for them during those months anyway.

Now, don't you feel better just knowing that the garage can be cleaned and organized? Then get your calendar out, call the family together, and decide when!

Chapter 13

Sewing and Crafts Solutions

"She has no fear of winter for her household, for she has made warm clothes for all of them. She also upholsters with finest tapestry; her own clothing is beautifully made."

PROVERBS 31:21,22 TLB

*T*oday's creative women find their closets, drawers, and bedrooms filled with the clutter of craft items, patterns, fabrics, straw flowers, glue guns, and fiberfill. It would be wonderful to have a room devoted exclusively to sewing and crafts. However, most of us must make do with a corner of the bedroom, living room, or even the garage. Piles of clutter can overwhelm us and the family. How can we organize all of this mess and retrieve any item quickly when needed? It's really very simple.

Here are the tools you need to solve the problem:

- Several "perfect boxes" for storage. Or if you prefer, use plastic bins, laundry baskets, plastic stacking trays, or wooden boxes.

- Several small jars (baby food style)

- 3" x 5" cards

- Pen

- Shoe boxes

If you've read the total-mess-to-total-rest chapter, you'll recognize some of the process. You can add boxes of craft and sewing items to your storage, listing them by number on 3" x 5" cards in the "Storage" section of your card file. This is a simple and fast way of retrieving items quickly.

Let's take your patterns. They can be organized and stored according to size and types—play clothes, dressy outfits, costumes, sport clothing, blouses, pants, etc. Many fabric stores carry cardboard boxes made specifically for storing patterns, and their cost is low.

The process is the same for fabrics. Put them in piles according to color: prints, solids, stripes, etc. Then place each pile on a separate cardboard "perfect box," number the box, and fill out a corresponding 3" x 5" card. Your cards might look something like this:

Box 1—Calico fabrics
      Reds and pinks

Box 2—Solid fabrics
      Blues, browns, blacks

Box 3—Stripes, polka dots

Box 4—Remnants and scraps, a yard or less

Repeat the process with arts and craft items. Now for some more ideas for organizing all those buttons, pins, hook, snaps. . . .

   • Organize buttons on safety pins, pipe cleaners, or twist ties. Or stick loose buttons and snaps on strips of transparent tape.

   • Store bias tape, piping, and hem tape in a shoebox. Don't forget to clearly label the box.

   • Store hook and eyes, snaps, and buttons in baby food jars. They will look so organized when lined on a shelf, or even when stored in shoeboxes (appropriately labeled, of course!).

• If you don't have a bobbin box, string bobbins on pipe cleaners or keep them in a plastic ice cube tray or egg carton. This is also a great way to store safety pins, buttons, and other miscellaneous small items.

• To organize spools of thread, group them according to color and lay them on their sides in a drawer or in shoebox tops. Stack the box tops so that the most frequently used colors are on top.

• Discarded shoeboxes are great for storing sewing supplies and smaller arts and crafts items. Be sure you label the boxes so you know their contents.

• Fabric fill or stuffing and quilting materials can be stored in cardboard "perfect boxes" using the numbering system. So can straw and silk flowers and other such items.

• For craft projects, a hot glue gun is terrific. Be sure to unplug it when not in use and store it out of the reach of children. Let it cool before placing it in its storage area.

• Egg cartons are good organizers. The small compartments are great for pins, small craft items, paper clips, stamps, etc.

• Clamp pattern pieces together with a clothespin until you finish the project and return them to the envelope.

• Large manila envelopes are also great for organization and storage. The contents can be listed on the outside and stored in "perfect boxes" or a drawer. Items you might store this way are: fabric scraps, ribbons, pipe cleaners, lace, bias tape, elastic, zippers, and stencils.

• Baskets are also a fun way to store arts and craft materials. You might consider putting several craft items in a basket and giving it as a Christmas gift to a friend.

• Another gift idea is to spray glue on a "perfect box" and cover it with a patchwork of fabric pieces. It looks country and creative. In fact, you might even do it for yourself! It would be a good way to quickly see what fabrics you've stored in the box.

Now that you're all organized, you don't have to spend half your time finding supplies and setting up. You can devote your energies to what you do best— creating!

Part III

Survival Through Organized Children

Child-Proof Safety in the Home

*I*t was early December and we were decorating our mantel for Christmas. We had just placed our handsome wooden goose, which weighs about 25 pounds, on our sturdy wood mantel. Who would have expected he could jump off and land on my right foot! The goose was repaired in a few minutes. We put a bow around his neck and placed him back in his spot. My foot? Well it took a little longer to fix—six weeks in a cast and six months before it was fully healed.

The moral of the story—don't tangle with a wooden goose! Even when we take precautions, accidents can happen. The National Safety Council estimates there is a home accident every seven seconds. Many of them can be avoided.

Shortly after our two adorable grandchildren were born, I realized again the importance of making our home safe for small children. Even though we no longer have children living in our home, I don't want to take a chance of an accident when one of those precious grandchildren come for a visit. Charcoal lighter fluid might not

155

taste good, yet a thirsty child could easily grab the can, put it to his mouth, and down a swallow in a matter of seconds. So we all need to be aware and do a little organizing now to hopefully prevent any accidents to those we love.

Let's use the following as a checklist to child-proof our homes:

Kitchen

• Keep knives in knife holders on a wall or in a high drawer.

• Place knives point down in the dishwasher.

• Cleaning powders and solutions can be stored in a plastic bucket or carryall with handle and stored on a shelf in the garage or hall closet. This can then be taken from room to room to clean, and frees up space under the kitchen and bathroom sinks for storing towels and paper products.

• Never leave a cord plugged into a socket when the other end is exposed. That's an open invitation for a baby to place the cord in his mouth.

• Use an empty toilet paper tube to store your cords, placing them in a drawer.

• When cooking on a stove top, keep handles facing the back of the stove. Children can easily dump boiling water or hot food on themselves by pulling an exposed handle or swinging a toy overhead. (Incidentally, the best way I've found to treat minor burns is to run cold water over them. Blisters don't usually appear. Raw egg whites are also good to rub on burns.)

• Always wrap broken glass in paper or place it in an old paper sack before throwing it in the trash. This is also a good rule for razor blades and the lids from metal cans.

It protects a child who might inadvertently drop a toy in the trash and try to retrieve it. Or the explorer who can't just dump the trash but has to check out every item in the process.

• When cleaning broken glass off the floor, dampen a paper towel and it will wipe up all those little pieces of glass. It protects the hands, too.

• Teach children to pour hot water slowly, aiming the stream away from themselves. Be sure to check the lid of a teapot or kettle to make sure it fits tightly and won't fall into the cup and splash boiling water.

• Any poisonous or extremely hazardous products should be kept in a locked cabinet on a very high shelf.

• Don't store products in unlabeled jars or cans. It's too easy to forget what's inside.

• Put safety covers over every exposed electrical outlet. Small children love to stick fingers and objects into these openings. These plastic caps are very inexpensive and can be purchased at drug stores, hardware stores, and many children's shops.

Bathroom

• *Never, absolutely never leave children unattended in the bathtub.* A lifeguard needs to be on duty at *all* times. There are too many hazards the youngster faces. If the doorbell or phone rings, take the child with you—or don't answer it.

• Check water temperature before putting children in the tub or shower. It might have started out warm, but gotten hotter by inadvertently brushing the knob.

• Never allow children to fiddle with the faucets. Scalds happen very quickly.

• Never add hot water to the bathtub with baby in it. Make sure the hot water faucet is turned off tightly. Wrap a washcloth around the faucet for safety when a baby or young child is in the tub.

• Teach every family member that the shower valve is always turned OFF when finished. Otherwise a bather or bathtub cleaner risks getting scalding water on the head. (Not to mention the possibility of Mom ruining her hairdo.)

• When small children are running around the house, keep bathroom doors closed at all times. A latch placed above the knob will eliminate a major source of accidents.

• Be careful of bathroom doors that lock from the inside. Be sure you have an emergency key and know where to find it should Junior lock himself in.

• Door gates are also a good way to close off a bathroom, as well as other rooms and stairs. These gates can be purchased at most stores that have baby departments. Often you can find them at garage sales or through the classified ad section of your newspaper.

Shopping with the Kids

• Make sure toddlers and smaller children are secured in the shopping cart by a cloth belt or string rope. This prevents them from standing and risking a dangerous fall. Recently I found a quilted shopping cart liner at a boutique. It fits into the seat of the cart and has a tie to hold babies and toddlers in their seats. It's cute and functional. I gave it to our daughter to use for our grandchildren. Check in your pattern books to see if they've come out with the pattern.

• Don't let your little darlings run wild in a store. Also, don't let them push the shopping cart, unless you want them to run over people and bump into shelves, counters, and food cases.

• Children often want to help you shop. But that help should not take the form of pulling items off shelves. Especially the bottom container in a beautifully-stacked pyramid of cereal boxes.

• Cans can be a danger if dropped on a foot, especially a barefooted little person. Or a child inside a cart can pick up a can and drop it outside the cart—onto Mom's toe.

• Teach children not to nag for your attention, trying to get you to buy candy or a food item they saw on television. Reward children after shopping when they've been good—with some fruit, or feeding the ducks, or time with Mom to color, draw, or play a game.

Miscellaneous

• Post emergency phone numbers in plain view by the phone for you and babysitters.

• Take a first-aid class, including CPR (cardiopulmonary resuscitation), from your local Red Cross.

• Give children swimming lessons at the earliest possible age. Many YMCA's and YWCA's offer great programs for children. If lessons aren't available, work with your children on holding their breath and blowing bubbles under water. It's fun and it will help them become comfortable in water.

• Buy or make up a first-aid kit, if you don't already have one. This is stored out of children's reach.

• Use side rails on small children's beds to keep them from falling out. These can be purchased out of catalogs or in children's departments.

• Keep scissors, plastic bags, ice picks, shish kebab skewers, fondue forks, and matches out of the reach of children.

• Warn children never to touch an electrical appliance plug with wet hands.

For more safety ideas, see *Emilie's Household Hints*, published by Harvest House Publishers.

Chapter 15

Family Conference Time

"Be subject to one another in the fear of Christ."

EPHESIANS 5:21 NASB

*P*robably the number one question women ask me at the More Hours in My Day seminars is, "How do I get my husband and children involved?"

That's a difficult question to answer because each family is different. However, in this day of changing roles in our society, it is very important that we have a common understanding within our families about what needs to be accomplished, and who will do it. Most of us no longer live in a time when Mom takes care of the inside of the house and Dad takes care of earning the money. Conflict arises when we don't recognize that changes are taking place.

One mistake many women make is that they assume everyone understands his or her roles. They never discuss their expectations with their husband or children. With many mothers working, it is often necessary for other family members to assume some of the responsibilities that once were traditionally the woman's. The family needs to understand the concept of *team*. Discipline, sacrifice, and investment of time are required as team members strive to "win." The coach and captain aren't the only players that make a winning team. Mom isn't the only player in the family—everyone has a valuable part. So I first recommend that moms stop carrying the whole team. That only leads to tired, burned-out, frustrated women.

It didn't take the Barnes family long to realize we needed a regular, set time to discuss important topics. Since one of our long-range goals was to raise independent children who were responsible teenagers, Bob and I felt one way to achieve this goal was to allow them to be part of the decision-making process. When someone is allowed to help make decisions, he or she is more likely to share the responsibility.

But how could we set aside more time when everyone was already busy with many activities? Our solution also resolved another chronic problem in our home. Probably the most hectic time for our family was Sunday morning before church. Mom and Dad often had a few cross words because we were late. Breakfast was hurried. Mom couldn't get dressed until the children's hair was combed. The children were crying because of a disagreement. By the time we drove into the church parking lot, we were rarely in a mood for worship. All in all, Sundays were strained times.

In order to solve our two problems—stressful Sundays and the need for family meetings—we decided to start going out for breakfast on Sunday mornings before church. Overnight we saw an improvement. This eliminated the problem of food preparation and cleanup. It was an opportunity to teach our children the social graces. And it gave us time to discuss various aspects of our family life. We established Sunday breakfasts as part of our regular monthly budget, and all of us looked forward to these times together.

Over the years, we changed our family meetings from Sunday breakfasts to Friday evening activities, and then back again to Sunday breakfasts. Mom and Dad often discussed topics to be reviewed beforehand, but there was also opportunity for any child to place a specific item on the agenda. This process helped our family become a team.

These meetings were often opened to friends. We let our children take turns inviting a friend to join our family. This gave us an opportunity to meet our children's friends and allowed them to meet us. Occasionally a whole family would join us. This was a great time to share our Christian faith, and often they were our guests at church.

Sometimes we planned various family activities at these breakfasts. While we continued the eating out tradition, we could have accomplished the same goal in many other ways. Family conferences and fun can be combined in such activities as:

- Make a collage on love
- Make and fly kites
- Assemble puzzles
- Write and produce a play
- View family movies or videos
- have family celebrations
- Exercise together
- Have a make-up party
- Visit a local industry
- Have a fix-it night
- Make a terrarium
- Write letters to grandparents
- Cook and bake
- Make and sail a boat
- Play board games
- Tell stories
- Put on a puppet show
- Go on picnics
- Model clay
- Ride bicycles
- Play charades
- Visit a farm
- Have discussions and debates
- Have a fire drill
- Make Christmas ornaments
- Make candles

There are many more family activities; we're limited only by our imagination. Our family activities and conference times played a valuable part in establishing harmony, respect, and pride in our family unit. Not every meeting and activity was a success, but we usually gained greater respect for our family members. When the children got older, we often ended the time by having each person mention his or her needs so we could pray specifically for each other during the next week.

Family Work Planner

There is no reason why Mom must continue to pick up after everyone in the home. We had a motto in our family: "Anything you mess up, you clean up." This little saying saved all of us many hours of double duty, and gave us time to go camping, fishing, to the museum, or to the beach, rather than being strapped to the house on weekends.

One idea that helped us to distribute the workload around the house was to write on separate slips of paper the chores that needed to be done each week. We placed these slips in a basket and every Saturday each of us drew one or more slips and learned our responsibilities for the next week. As each assignment was drawn, it was recorded on a Daily Work Planner (see Exhibit U) which was posted in a conspicuous place. Each family member was responsible to complete his assignment. Mom and Dad also drew, for this was a team effort. Everyone helped meet the responsibilities of the family.

If you have a wide range of ages in your home, you might want to use two baskets—one for the smaller children and one for the rest of the family. That way the little children don't draw jobs that are too difficult. It is also important that Mom and Dad inspect to make sure the chores are done properly. Remember, "It's not what you expect, but what you inspect" that teaches children to be responsible family members. Occasionally, to help

DAILY WORK PLANNER

DATE March 23-29

DAY OF WEEK	MOM	DAD	#1 CHILD	#2 CHILD	#3 CHILD	#4 CHILD	#5 CHILD
SATURDAY	- Clean out the garage — McDonalds - 6:00PM						Feed Dog
SUNDAY	Church - Family						
MONDAY	Laundry		Clean bedrm.			Fold Clothes	Feed Dog
TUESDAY	ironing	set out trash	Rake leaves	Rake leaves	Rake leaves		
WEDNESDAY	House Work		Vacuum House			Dust w/Mom	
THURSDAY		Wash Car		Help wash Car			
FRIDAY	Laundry	set out trash	Mow lawn	sweep walk-ways	water plants		

EXHIBIT U

build good team morale, give a special reward if the children have done a good job for several weeks.

Please note that I am not suggesting that children assume the load in maintaining a house. As parents we must be sensitive to our children's own activities. They need time to participate in sports, music, homework, and other school and church activities. We want to let them experience being a child. At the same time, there are responsibilities that they have as members of a family. We need to work together so no one family member has too heavy a load.

Sometimes the family unit has to pitch in for special occasions—when company is coming, cleaning the garage, a garage sale, etc. Sometimes one family member's needs are more important than the others at that time. We need to learn to make those value judgments, and we can by being sensitive to the needs of everyone in the family.

We also need to recognize our priorities in relating to our mate and children. When my children were still at home, I often remembered, "You were a wife to your husband before you were a mother to your children." The children will grow up and leave home (hopefully). However, we will still have our mates. We don't want to wake up one morning after the children are raised and think, "Who am I?" So a couple needs to spend quality time with each other without the children. We must nor use the excuse that we can't afford it. We can't afford not to. Bob and I have planned times together and put them on our calendar just as we would any other appointment. We protect those times and don't cancel unless there is a real emergency.

For single women who are raising children alone, the pressures are even more intense, especially when children are young. I believe the family conference time and division of responsibilities can help relieve some of the pressure. However sometimes as women, whether married or single, we may have to leave some things undone rather than continue to tax our own spirit and become burned-out. One question we can learn to ask is "Will it matter in five years?" If not, maybe it's not that important today.

There are no rules on how a home should be run. Each family needs to set its own standards. My family has loved working together as we set joint goals. But it's a process that takes time and everyone must learn new ways of cooperating.

Chapter 16

Babysitting Survival Guide

> *"I will instruct you and teach you in the way which you should go; I will counsel you with My eye upon you."*
>
> PSALM 32:8 NASB

Sixteen-year-old Lynn arrived at the Merrihew home eager to take care of Craig and Jenny's two adorable toddlers. The three of them talked briefly, then Craig and Jenny practically skipped out the door, delighted to have their first "date" in six weeks.

Forty-five minutes later, two-year-old Christine was still crying and screaming "Mommy!" Lynn remembered that Craig and Jenny were going to three different places that evening, but couldn't remember when they would be there. She wasn't even sure if she should call. Meanwhile, Craig and Jenny kept remembering things they wished they'd told Lynn. Their intimate conversation was interrupted by an ongoing debate about whether or not they should call home.

Whether our babysitter is 16 or 66, there are certain things we can do to insure a smoother and more enjoyable evening for both sitter and parents.

For Mom and Dad

- Leave a pad and pen by the phone so the sitter can

note phone messages and information about the evening's events.

• Have a first-time sitter arrive a few minutes early so you and your children can get acquainted with him or her. Also, give her a brief tour of the pertinent parts of the house—children's rooms, bathroom, location of TV, location of first-aid and other supplies.

• Explain home rules about snacking, visitors, use of television or stereo, etc.

• Tell sitter what time each child goes to bed, and whether a child has a special routine—a favorite story to be read, a special blanket, a prayer time. Better yet, put these instructions in writing and keep them handy for each sitter.

• If necessary, show sitter procedures for feeding, warming bottle, and changing diapers.

• If a child is taking medication, leave a measuring spoon or dropper and written instructions concerning time and dosage next to the bottle.

• Let a sitter know at the time of initial contact whether he or she will be expected to prepare and serve a meal.

• Have a flashlight or candle handy in case of power failure.

• If the sitter cannot easily reach you, plan to call home periodically.

• If you are unable to arrive home when you said you would, call and let the sitter know you will be late and when to expect you.

• Always be prepared to pay the sitter the previously-agreed-upon fee when you return home, unless you have worked out some other arrangement ahead of time. Remember that checks are sometimes hard for teenagers to cash. Some parents pay extra for hours after midnight.

• If you must cancel a sitter at the last minute, it is courteous to pay the sitter for part of the time they were expected to sit.

• If you want the sitter to do any housework, make special arrangements at the time you hire her. Most parents pay extra for such service.

You might want to make up a printed information sheet for your sitters. Exhibit V is one idea for such a sheet. It has room for emergency phone numbers and special instructions as well as a place for the sitter to leave any comments about the evening.

As far as what is expected from a sitter, you might want to photocopy these and give them to a new sitter before you hire her.

For the Babysitter

• Be sure you understand what is expected of you. Don't count on your memory; write down instructions if the list gets too long.

• Be sure you know where the parents or other adults such as grandparents or an aunt or uncle can be reached at all times.

• It is best if the children are present when parents give you instructions so everyone understands the rules.

• Don't open the door for strangers.

• Keep outside doors locked at all times.

• Deliveries can be left outside, or delivered later when parents are home.

• Never tell phone-callers that parents are not at home. Take a message, if possible.

• Keep your own phone calls brief.

BABY-SITTER'S INFORMATION SHEET

We can be reached at: ⎯⎯⎯⎯⎯⎯⎯⎯⎯⎯⎯⎯⎯⎯⎯⎯⎯⎯⎯⎯⎯⎯⎯⎯⎯

We will be home about ⎯⎯⎯⎯⎯⎯⎯⎯⎯⎯⎯ **o' clock.**

A little about us:

    Our name: ⎯⎯⎯⎯⎯⎯⎯⎯⎯⎯⎯⎯⎯⎯⎯⎯⎯⎯⎯⎯⎯⎯⎯⎯⎯⎯⎯⎯

    Our address: ⎯⎯⎯⎯⎯⎯⎯⎯⎯⎯⎯⎯⎯⎯⎯⎯⎯⎯⎯⎯⎯⎯⎯⎯⎯⎯⎯

    Our phone number: ⎯⎯⎯⎯⎯⎯⎯⎯⎯⎯⎯⎯⎯⎯⎯⎯⎯⎯⎯⎯⎯⎯⎯

    Children's names: ⎯⎯⎯⎯⎯⎯⎯⎯⎯⎯⎯⎯⎯⎯⎯⎯⎯⎯⎯⎯⎯⎯⎯⎯

    Ages: ⎯⎯⎯⎯⎯⎯⎯⎯⎯⎯⎯⎯⎯⎯⎯⎯⎯⎯⎯⎯⎯⎯⎯⎯⎯⎯⎯⎯⎯⎯⎯

Emergency numbers:

    Doctor: ⎯⎯⎯⎯⎯⎯⎯⎯⎯⎯⎯⎯⎯⎯⎯⎯⎯⎯⎯⎯⎯⎯⎯⎯⎯⎯⎯⎯⎯

    Dentist: ⎯⎯⎯⎯⎯⎯⎯⎯⎯⎯⎯⎯⎯⎯⎯⎯⎯⎯⎯⎯⎯⎯⎯⎯⎯⎯⎯⎯⎯

    Police: ⎯⎯⎯⎯⎯⎯⎯⎯⎯⎯⎯⎯⎯⎯⎯⎯⎯⎯⎯⎯⎯⎯⎯⎯⎯⎯⎯⎯⎯⎯

    Fire/Rescue: ⎯⎯⎯⎯⎯⎯⎯⎯⎯⎯⎯⎯⎯⎯⎯⎯⎯⎯⎯⎯⎯⎯⎯⎯⎯⎯

    Poison Control: ⎯⎯⎯⎯⎯⎯⎯⎯⎯⎯⎯⎯⎯⎯⎯⎯⎯⎯⎯⎯⎯⎯⎯⎯

    Neighbor: ⎯⎯⎯⎯⎯⎯⎯⎯⎯⎯⎯⎯⎯⎯⎯⎯⎯⎯⎯⎯⎯⎯⎯⎯⎯⎯⎯

Special Instructions:

- Location of thermostat ⎯⎯⎯⎯⎯⎯⎯⎯⎯⎯⎯⎯⎯⎯⎯⎯⎯⎯⎯⎯
- Instructions about pets ⎯⎯⎯⎯⎯⎯⎯⎯⎯⎯⎯⎯⎯⎯⎯⎯⎯⎯⎯⎯
- Location of children's food and clothing ⎯⎯⎯⎯⎯⎯⎯⎯⎯⎯⎯

⎯⎯⎯⎯⎯⎯⎯⎯⎯⎯⎯⎯⎯⎯⎯⎯⎯⎯⎯⎯⎯⎯⎯⎯⎯⎯⎯⎯⎯⎯⎯⎯⎯⎯⎯⎯

- Children's habits ⎯⎯⎯⎯⎯⎯⎯⎯⎯⎯⎯⎯⎯⎯⎯⎯⎯⎯⎯⎯⎯⎯⎯⎯

⎯⎯⎯⎯⎯⎯⎯⎯⎯⎯⎯⎯⎯⎯⎯⎯⎯⎯⎯⎯⎯⎯⎯⎯⎯⎯⎯⎯⎯⎯⎯⎯⎯⎯⎯⎯

- Bedtime/Naptime ⎯⎯⎯⎯⎯⎯⎯⎯⎯⎯⎯⎯⎯⎯⎯⎯⎯⎯⎯⎯⎯⎯⎯⎯

⎯⎯⎯⎯⎯⎯⎯⎯⎯⎯⎯⎯⎯⎯⎯⎯⎯⎯⎯⎯⎯⎯⎯⎯⎯⎯⎯⎯⎯⎯⎯⎯⎯⎯⎯⎯

Children behaved:

⎯⎯⎯⎯⎯⎯⎯Above Average

⎯⎯⎯⎯⎯⎯⎯Average

⎯⎯⎯⎯⎯⎯⎯Needs Improvement

Comments: ⎯⎯⎯⎯⎯⎯⎯⎯⎯⎯⎯⎯⎯⎯⎯⎯⎯⎯⎯⎯⎯⎯⎯⎯⎯⎯

⎯⎯⎯⎯⎯⎯⎯⎯⎯⎯⎯⎯⎯⎯⎯⎯⎯⎯⎯⎯⎯⎯⎯⎯⎯⎯⎯⎯⎯⎯⎯⎯⎯⎯⎯⎯

⎯⎯⎯⎯⎯⎯⎯⎯⎯⎯⎯⎯⎯⎯⎯⎯⎯⎯⎯⎯⎯⎯⎯⎯⎯⎯⎯⎯⎯⎯⎯⎯⎯⎯⎯⎯

⎯⎯⎯⎯⎯⎯⎯⎯⎯⎯⎯⎯⎯⎯⎯⎯⎯⎯⎯⎯⎯⎯⎯⎯⎯⎯⎯⎯⎯⎯⎯⎯⎯⎯⎯⎯

EXHIBIT V

• Always clean up your own messes. The extra effort you make will encourage the parents to call you again.

• Don't snoop in closets or drawers. Even though you are working in the home, you are still a guest.

• Try to stay alert and awake unless it is a long, late evening.

• Let parents know of any illness or accident, however minor. Accidents will happen and most parents allow for this.

• If you have to cancel, let parents know as soon as possible.

• It's a good idea to take a first-aid course at your local YWCA, Red Cross, or community service department. Some cities have regular classes designed for babysitters. If yours doesn't, buy a first-aid handbook.

Chapter 17

Teach Your Children About Money

"Train up a child in the way he should go, even when he is old he will not depart from it."

PROVERBS 22:6 NASB

*W*e live in a world where adults find themselves in financial woes. We learn about money usually by trial and error. Few families take the time to teach their children how to be smart with money. Yet at an early age, children know about money and what it can do for them.

Children who learn about money at an early age will be ahead of this mystery game. Learning to deal with money properly will foster discipline, good work habits, and self-respect.

Below you will find several ways you can help your children get a good handle on money.

1. *Start with an allowance.* Most experts advise that an allowance should not be tied directly to a child's daily chores. Children should help around the home not because they get paid for it, but because they share responsibilities as members of a family. However, you might pay a child for doing extra jobs at home. This can develop their initiative. We know of parents who give stickers to their children when they help around the house without having to be asked. At the child's discretion

they may redeem the stickers for 25 cents each. This has been a great motivator not only for initiative but also for teaching teamwork in the family.

An allowance is a vital tool for teaching children how to budget, save, and make their own decisions. Children remember and learn from mistakes when their own money is lost or spent foolishly.

How large an allowance to give depends upon your individual status. The amount should be based upon developing a fair budget that allows for entertainment, snacks, lunch money, bus fare, and school supplies. Add some extra money for contributing to the church and savings. Be willing to hold your children responsible for living within their budget. Some weeks they may have to go without, particularly when they run out of money.

2. *Model the proper use of credit.* In today's society we see the results of individuals and couples using bad judgment regarding credit. Explain to children why it's necessary to use credit and the importance of paying their loan back on a timely basis. You can make this a great teaching tool. Give them practice in filling out credit forms. Their first loan might be from you to them for a special purchase. Go through all the mechanics that a bank would do: Fill out a credit application; sign a paper with all the information stated. Let them understand about interest, installment payments, balloon payments, late payment costs, etc. Teach them to be responsible about paying on time.

3. *Teach your children how to save.* In today's instant society, it is hard to teach this lesson. At times we should deny our children certain material things so they have a reason to save. As they get older they will want bicycles, stereos, a car, a big trip, etc. They can relate to establishing the habit of saving with these larger items.

One of the first ways to begin teaching the concept of savings is to give the children a form of piggy bank. This way spare change or extra earnings can go into the piggy bank. When the bank gets full, you might want to open an account at the local bank.

When they are older you might want to establish a passbook account at the local bank so they can go to the bank and personally deposit to their account. Most banks will not pay interest until the balance becomes larger, but this helps the children begin thinking about savings.

In the end, children who learn how to save will better appreciate what they've worked to acquire.

4. *Show them how to be wise in their spending.* Take your children with you when you shop and do some cost comparisons. They will soon see that with a little effort they can save a lot of money. You might want to show them in a tangible way when they want to purchase a larger item for themselves. Go to several stores looking for that one item. Write down the most expensive and the least expensive amount for the same item. Let them choose which one they want to purchase and pay them the difference between what they chose and the most expensive. This way they can really see the savings.

Clothes is an area where a lot of lessons on wise spending can be made. After a while children realize that designer clothes cost a lot more for that label or patch. Our daughter Jenny soon learned that outlet stores were a great place to find bargains for clothes dollars. To this day she can still find excellent bargains by comparison shopping.

5. *Let children work part-time.* There are many excellent part-time jobs waiting for your child. Working in fast-food outlets, markets and malls, or babysitting, etc. gives valuable work experience to your children. Some entrepreneurial youngsters even begin a thriving business around their skills and interests. These part-time jobs are real confidence boosters. Just remember to keep

a proper balance between work, home, church, and school. A limit of 10–15 hours per week might be a good guideline. Much more than that will affect a proper balance.

6. *Let them help you with your expenses.* Encourage your children to help you budget and pay for the family expenses. This gives them experience in real-life money problems. They also get a better idea regarding your family's financial income and expenses.

Children's ideas are good when it comes to suggestions about how we can better utilize family finances. This will give them a better understanding of why your family can't afford certain luxuries.

7. *Give them experience in handling adult expenses.* As your children get older they need to experience real-life costs. Since children live at home, they don't always share in true-to-life expenses. Let them experience paying for their own telephone, car expenses, and clothing expenses. Depending upon the situation, help in paying a portion of the utility and household bills would be an invaluable experience for children who have left school and are still living at home.

8. *Give unto the Lord.* At a very young stage in life, parents and children should talk about where things we have come from. The children should be aware that all things are given by God and He is just letting us borrow them for a time. Children can understand that we are to return back to God what He has so abundantly given to us. This principle can be experienced either through their Sunday school or church offerings. When special projects at church come up, you might want to review the needs with your children so they can decide if they want to give extra monies above what they normally give to their church. Early training in this area gives a valuable basis for learning how to be a giver in life and not a taker.

Your children will learn about money from you. Be a good model. As they get older they will imitate what you do. If you have good habits, they will reflect that. If you struggle with finances, so will they. One valuable lesson to teach is that money doesn't reflect love. A hug, a smile, a kiss, or time spent together is much more valuable than money. *You set the example!*

Chapter 18

Smart Ideas for Parents— That Work!

> "When God measures a man, he puts the tape around the heart, not around the head."
>
> AUTHOR UNKNOWN

*A*s many women come to my seminars, they not only ask about ideas that they can use with their children, but many times they share with me ideas that work in their families. It's great when children beg to do an activity that has been so successful with the family.

The Special Red Plate

When we honor someone in our family with our red plate which reads "You Are Special Today," their eyes light up and a broad smile appears. This plate is used to honor birthdays, anniversaries, graduations, promotions, good grades, and many other celebrations. As part of the celebration, our family takes time to go around the table and share why the honored guest is "special." What joy when a teenage brother tells why his teenage sister is special! We are to honor our family members at all times. After we have all shared with our honored guest, that person gets to share with us why he or she is special. We have had the recipients turn to tears as they hear members of the family share with them face-to-face.

181

Many times we don't take time to share with members of the family the positive aspects of life. This plate really helps accentuate the positive.

"I Love You Because" Cards

A small card that reads "I Love You Because..." is another tool we use to tell our family members that we love them. A typical card might read, "Dear Brad, I love you because you come to the table each morning with a smile," or "Dear Christine, I love you because you take good care of your dog and cat." These make great place cards for dinner guests. Many times this has been the first time in a long time that someone has expressed love to them. I also tuck cards into lunch pails or even Bob's attaché when he's away from me on a trip as just a touch from home.

Yogurt Run

Our one goal as moms is to get our children into bed on a regular time schedule, but on weekends or while on vacation you might try this little idea that breaks away from the normal routine. When the children are all tucked in for a good night's sleep, go into their bedroom, flip on the light, and with a delightful voice express, "Yogurt run." Then bundle the children up, pack them in the car, and drive to your nearest yogurt store. The children will think that Mom and/or Dad have zoned out, but they will never forget this special outing. In fact, they will soon ask, "When can we have a yogurt run again?"

"I Was Caught Being Good"

This little sticker has been one of the best motivators

for our grandchildren. Many parents and teachers have noticed great positive effects for those children who receive them.

As children are caught being good, they are given a sticker which tells everyone around them that they did something good. They wear it proudly. Soon after seeing the sticker, brother or sister will come up and ask, "What did Bevan do to get a sticker?" After sharing what was done, the other children start looking for things they can do to get caught being good. It really works, and the children are recognized for their positive contributions to the family. We also go one step further by taking the sticker from them at the day's end and placing it on a sheet of paper with the child's name at the top. After accumulating ten stickers, the children can turn their stickers in for a one-dollar bill. This is a great motivator to continue doing good. Catch your children doing something good and praise them, praise them, praise them.

Just Like Dad or Granddad

Kids want to be just like Dad (or Granddad). When they come in the bathroom with Dad while he is shaving, spread a washcloth on the toilet seat, fill the cap from the can of shaving cream with some of the foam, give each child a small household brush, and let the little shaver have a fun time.

Money Management

To teach your school-age child about managing money, try this. Give them money to buy lunch at the school. Tell them if they decide to take their lunch from home and if they pack it themselves, they are allowed to spend their lunch money on whatever they want. They will become good at planning their lunches and deciding on how they want to budget their money.

Mirror, Mirror on the Wall

If your daily wrestling match with your children to get their clothes on without tiring you out is getting old, you might try dressing them in front of a full-length mirror. The mirror allows them to see what is going on, making them feel like a participant rather than an unwilling victim.

Family Photo Album

It used to be that we all had many of our family members living around our homes, but today's family members are located all over the country. It is often hard for youngsters to associate a name with a face. Make up a special "family" photo album and periodically thumb through it with your child, talking about Uncle Bill and Aunt Betty. This way your child will not just see a face but will have a clear picture of who the face belongs to.

No Ghosts on the Ceiling

If it's hard for your children to get to sleep at night because they lie awake thinking scary thoughts, try a "sweet dreams" box. Cut out colorful pictures of animals, toys, children, etc. from old magazines and put them in a special box. Each night before your children go to bed, have them take a picture while falling to sleep to promote soothing thoughts for sleep time.

Clean Car Catchall

Place a dish-drain tray under your child's car seat. The tray catches crumbs, sand, grass, dirt from shoes, and liquid from spilled drinks. The tray is easily removed, keeps the floor and seats much neater, and makes cleaning easier.

Saved by the Bell

A kitchen timer can come in handy with your child. Time their bath or those last ten minutes before bedtime. This is also an excellent technique to time your time alone as Mom. Just tell the children, "Mommy is going to have her time until the bell goes off." When your child's friends come to play, avoid the question, "Do I have to go home yet?" by simply telling them that you are setting the timer to the time when they should stop playing. When friends come over to visit, one problem always occurs: They all want to play with the same toy or game. Use this timer and explain that each child can play with the favored toy for ten minutes before passing it to the next in line when the buzzer sounds.

Learn By Singing

Children learn much faster if they can put a tune to whatever is being learned. Set your address and phone numbers to the tune of one of your child's favorite nursery rhymes, and you'll find they won't have any problem memorizing this important information.

Wish Books

Madison Avenue has done a great job of teaching our

children to want everything which they see or hear about in the media. They want, want, want. Try making an "I wish" book from a large blank notebook. When your children see something they want, help them look through magazines and/or catalogs to find a picture of it. Cut the picture out and paste it in the book. When you go shopping for a special-occasion gift, take the book along. This way you are buying items that the children (and other family members) want.

Creative Gifts

You don't need to spend a lot of time or money for that special children's gift. Try one with a little imagination:

- A recording of their most-requested fairy story or book—in your own voice.
- A book to keep stickers in
- A poster of your child's favorite hero
- Ten "coupons" that excuse your child from one chore a day
- A promise for your child to have a slumber party on a special date
- A coupon giving permission to use the car a certain number of times

Bags Full of Love

Here's a special, affordable gift for older children to give to a younger sister or brother: With colored markers, a few stickers, and a lot of love and patience, they can decorate lunch bags with rainbows, flowers, favorite cartoon heroes or adventures, incorporating the younger child's name into each design.

Round-the-Table Discussion

Things can be so very pessimistic in the family, and table talk can be a downer. One good discussion item is to say, "What's the best thing that happened to you today?" Give each family member an opportunity to share the best of the day. An additional benefit is to learn more about what's happening outside of the home. Sometimes these discussions are short and to the point, and sometimes they are strung out for 20–30 minutes. Be positive and uplifting at mealtime. (By the way, no TV on during this time.)

A Positive Scrapbook

Another uplifter to overcome that negative influence in our lives is to help your children buy and make a pretty fabric-covered journal in which to record happy events. Every night before bedtime, sit down together and recollect the "good things" that happened that day. They can then enter each item in their journal. This little exercise can help them to look more positively at a variety of situations.

Toe the Mark

If you are concerned for your children's safety because they are sitting too close to the TV set during viewing, put tape on the floor to mark the safe distance and have them sit behind that line.

Stay in Touch

To keep in touch with grandparents who are away

from you and the family, give children a tape recorder. By tape they can talk to relatives regularly and tell them what's happening in their lives. The children can tell about the big firsts in their lives. Even young children can give a message or song. The grandparents can tape the children's favorite stories, just talk to them, or send a special message for birthdays and Christmas.

Newspaper Caper

There are times when adults want to read the morning newspaper, the children want special attention, and we have morning hassles. One solution is to remove the comics section from the paper, roll and tie it, and present it to your children as their "very own" paper. Children also like to search the newspaper for food discount coupons that Mom can use when she goes to the market. As an incentive, you might offer them a percentage of the monies they save from the coupons they cut from the paper.

Be organized when dealing with your children. Well-planned strategies help reduce stress in your life and certainly give more stability in a confusing environment. Get in the habit of jotting down good ideas that work for other parents. Not all ideas work in every family, but step out and try something new. The children love newness to the typical routines of the family.

Part IV

Survival Through Organized Moving

Chapter 19

You're Moving... Again?

> "Lord, help me to realize how brief my time on earth will be. Help me to know that I am here for but a moment more."
>
> PSALM 39:4 TLB

My friend Marcia is married to a lieutenant in the U.S. Army. About the time she finally unpacks the last box and begins to feel somewhat acclimated to her new home, her husband announces, "It's time to pack up. We're moving next month." In the past 11 years, Marcia has moved 11 times.

Most women find the prospect of moving about as exciting as changing several messy diapers each day. It's usually not something we're eager to do. However, the fact is that most of us move on an average of once every three years. So it is a part of many of our lives. And if we're preplanned and organized, moving can be a fairly easy and smooth process.

Before we review our checklist, there are two questions we must have answered:

1) How long do we have to plan our move? Is it a week? A month? Six months? Our checklist can be adjusted to any time frame, but with a shorter period we need to set more rigid deadlines for each aspect of the list.

2) How are we going to move? Will this be a "do it ourselves" move, or will we hire a moving company, or do a combination of both?

Once we've established when and how we're moving, we are ready to begin.

Step 1: Household Check-Off List

There are so many details to remember before moving time that it's easy to forget important things until it's too late. There are essential details that should be taken care of before the moving van arrives.

Transfer of Records
- School records
- Auto registration
- Driver's license
- Bank accounts
- Medical and dental records
- Eyeglass and contact prescriptions
- Pet immunization records
- Legal documents
- Church and other organization memberships
- Insurance

Services to Discontinue
- Telephone
- Electric, gas, water, and other utilities
- Layaway purchases
- Cleaners—pick up all your clothes before the move

- Milk delivery
- Fuel delivery
- Cable television
- Pest control
- Water softener or bottled water
- Garbage pickup
- Diaper service

Change of Address Notification
- Local post office
- Magazines
- Friends and relatives
- Insurance companies
- Creditors and charge accounts
- Lawyer
- Church

Step 2: Preparing for Moving Day

- Reserve a moving company, if needed.
- Enlist some volunteers for moving day. Neighbors or friends from the church are potential candidates and usually are very willing to help.
- Collect boxes from local supermarkets and drugstores. Be sure to go to stores early in the day before boxes are flattened and tossed. Or ask the manager to save you a few boxes. Some moving companies will loan you special containers such as wardrobe boxes. "Perfect boxes" are also great for moving because they are standardized and have handles for easy lifting.
- Buy felt-tip marking pens to color-code your boxes. (More about this later.)

• Prepare a work area, such as a card table, that can be used for wrapping and packing.

• Clean and air out the refrigerator and kitchen range.

• Make sure gas appliances are properly disconnected.

• Make a list of items that require special care when being packed—your antique lamp, or a china cup and saucer collection.

• Empty gas tanks on mowers and chain saws and discard all flammable materials.

• Leave an open space in the driveway or on the street for the truck, trailer, or moving van.

• Keep a small box of tools handy to dismantle furniture.

• Keep a bucket, rags, and cleaning products ready for a final cleaning of the home after it is empty.

Step 3: Packing

This is probably the most important part of your move. Proper packing and identification of your containers can assure that none of your belongings are damaged or lost.

• Use sturdy boxes for packing. Fruit and liquor boxes often have extra reinforcement and are good for heavy items like books. In addition, have a generous supply of padding. Packing paper can be purchased at low cost at your local newspaper plant or a local moving company. This unprinted paper is excellent for wrapping dishes and glassware. (Ink from newspapers will stain many of your items.)

• Begin packing, if possible, two weeks before moving day.

• Use colored pens or a number system to mark each box, identifying its contents and the room where it is to go. Examples:

Yellow—Kitchen

Green—Garden and garage

Blue—Brad's bedroom

Or number boxes and make out 3" x 5" cards, using the system we described in Chapter 8. Make out one card for every box, and list on the card what is in the box and in which room it belongs. Put your cards in a small box to carry with you to your new home. There you can direct each box to the appropriate room by quick reference to the box number and your cards.

Because you know by your numbered cards what is in each box without opening the box, you can unpack priority items first. This is also a great way to organize things you plan on storing in the basement or attic of your new home.

• Moving is a good way to weed out things you no longer need or use. While some items should be thrown away, others such as old clothing can be donated to churches, orphanages, or the Salvation Army. Or if you have time, run an ad in the local paper, or hold a garage sale. Remember that when you give items away to non-profit organizations, you can use the net value as a deduction from your income tax. Be sure to get a signed receipt.

• Don't put fragile and heavy items together in the same box.

• Use smaller boxes for heavier items and larger boxes for lightweight, bulky items.

• Fill each box completely and compactly. Don't over or under fill.

• When packing glass dishes, put a paper plate between each plate as a protector. Stack plates on end—not flat. They seem to travel better packed that way.

• Popcorn (not the real kind) is another good packaging agent for china cups and crystal glasses. Fill the cups and glasses with popcorn before wrapping in unprinted paper. Foam padding also works well to protect breakables.

• To protect mirrors and paintings, cut heavy cardboard to fit around them, bind with tape, and label "FRAGILE."

• Remove legs, if possible, from table tops and pack them on edge. If that is not feasible, load tables with their surface down and legs up. Protect a wood finish with blankets or other padding.

• Furniture pads can be wrapped around items like lamps and tied together, or sewn together temporarily with heavy thread.

• Seal boxes with heavy-duty packing tape. Or put the boxes into trash bags and then tape.

• Move dresser drawers with the clothes inside.

• When removing medicines and cleaning agents from the bathroom, make sure they are packed and sealed immediately so small children cannot reach them.

Step 4: Loading the Van, Truck, or Trailer

• Park next to the widest door of your home, leaving enough room to extend a ramp.

• Load the vehicle one quarter section at a time, using all the space from floor to ceiling. Put heaviest items in the front half of the vehicle. Try to load weight evenly from side to side to prevent shifting.

• Tie off each quarter with rope. This prevents your items from banging against each other and keeps the load from shifting.

• Use a dolly for heavy items. This can be rented from a moving company or rental store.

• *Caution:* When lifting heavy objects, bend your knees and use your leg muscles. Keep your back as straight as possible.

• Fit bicycles and other odd-shaped items along the walls of the truck, or on top of stacked items.

• When everything is loaded, finish cleaning your house, lock the door, and you're on your way!

Step 5: Moving into Your New Home

The excitement of a new home is wonderful. It's kind of like a new beginning for the family. You get a chance to start afresh. You can put behind you those bad experiences with a neighbor, an animal, a child, a postman, or any number of experiences that weren't very favorable. True, you also leave behind some wonderful memories, experiences, and relationships—some which will be with you all your life.

Bob and I always took Brad and Jenny with us when looking at a new home. A move is a big adjustment for the whole family, not just for Mom and Dad. The children always wanted to see their new home, neighborhood, school, etc. If they know a little bit about the new situation, they are better members of the team and they can get excited along with you. Try to dispel as many of the "unknowns" as possible.

If you can arrive a few days before the moving van and can get access to the new home, set off a bug bomb or spray. (Even if you don't see bugs, there probably will be some, depending on the area and the season during which you will be moving. This way you won't worry about your family, your pets, foods, or furnishings during the spraying.)

If you are driving to your new home and you arrive late, spend the first night at a motel rather than trying to move in when everyone is tired. Everything will seem much more manageable come sunrise.

If you will arrive before the movers, you might want to bring along a good book, several magazines, a radio, or a portable television to "while away" the wait.

Try to have all the paperwork done for your new home *before* you move:

- Telephone installed
- Utilities connected
- Children enrolled in school, if possible (if not, be sure you have their latest report cards and/or transcripts handy when you enroll).

Bring a "survival package" so you can camp in your new home until the moving van arrives. You might include the following:

- Paper towels and clean rags
- Instant coffee or tea
- Coffeepot (if you like the real thing)
- Cups
- Utensils
- Soap and towels
- A can and bottle opener
- Candles
- A flashlight (make sure batteries are good)
- Some light bulbs
- Toilet paper
- Cleansing powder and window cleaner

- A first-aid kit
- Any daily medications that you and your family are taking

If you are transporting any animals, make sure they have water, food, and adequate ventilation. Don't leave your animals in the car during warm/hot days. The inside of your car can become a death trap for your animals if left alone for even a short period of time.

One technique that I use with our cat is to put butter on the bottom of her paws when we get to a new home. As she licks off the butter, she also licks off the smell of the old neighborhood, and she will stay around the new home better. (I would also recommend putting cats in an enclosed room or garage for the first two days.)

Depending upon the distance and mode of your move, be sure to bring along some books, games, and toys for the children. The trip will be much more pleasant if the children have some of their own activities along for the ride.

A messy backseat on a trip can be so distracting and discouraging. I used to spread out an old sheet over the backseat and floor of the car. When we would arrive at our rest stop, I would take out the sheet and dump the contents into a wastebasket. A clean area is easier to live with.

Chapter 20

Let's Have a Garage Sale!

"Any enterprise is built by wise planning, becomes strong through common sense, and profits wonderfully by keeping abreast of the facts."

PROVERBS 24:3,4 TLB

*T*he summer is almost over, the kids are restless, and you've had it with all the clutter. Why not plan a garage sale? Tell the kids they can keep the money from the sale of their items. You'll be amazed how quickly they are motivated to clean their rooms and get rid of clutter.

If you have school-age children at home, an annual garage sale is a must. It's the best way to motivate the family to clean out the garage, closets, and bedrooms. Most families are storing things they never use, taking up space in closets, shelves, cupboards, and under the bed.

When our kids lived at home, we'd talk about purchasing school supplies and new clothes a few weeks before school started. We'd make lists and estimate what it would cost to equip and outfit each child. That led naturally into planning our garage sale as a way to help finance back-to-school needs. We'd all get excited about the possibility of selling outgrown clothes, unused items, books, and old toys.

Back-to-school wasn't the only way to spend the money

we'd raise. We would discuss as a family other ways to use the money. Sometimes we agreed to give a portion to a missionary family, a church project, or the building fund. And the children would use some of the money they earned from selling their items to buy a new game or book they especially wanted. This was a great teaching tool to help them learn how to earn, give, spend, and save money.

Set the Date

It's best to make your garage sale for one day only, either on a Friday or Saturday.

Once the date is set, call the newspaper or community shopper and place an ad. The ad should be short. Do *not* include your phone number. It only produces a lot of unnecessary calls with silly questions. Here's a sample ad:

> GARAGE SALE—Saturday, September 6, 9:00 A.M. to 5:00 P.M. Bookcase, toys, antiques, appliances, clothing, bike, tools, and lots of goodies. 2838 Rumsey Drive, Central Avenue at Victoria

Now that you've placed the ad, you're committed. You've got to follow through and make it happen.

Making and Placing the Signs

Use heavy cardboard or brightly colored posterboard and bold felt-tip pens in contrasting colors. For example, if your board is yellow, use a black or dark blue pen.

Keep the signs simple. You don't need to list items. You only need the words GARAGE SALE in large letters, plus your street address. Many cars are like mine—they go on automatic when we see one of those signs—and before you know it, the car is parked right in front of that house.

Place your signs in prominent locations. Use your own stakes. Do not attach them to street or speed-limit signs. And when your sale is finished, always go back and remove the signs.

Deciding What to Sell

Now you need to clean house and decide what to sell. Spend time with each child and go over the items they begin to pull out of their rooms. Sometimes in the enthusiasm of the event, they decide to sell their bed, favorite teddy bear, even the cat or dog. You can help evaluate what goes, but be careful not to get too carried away yourself.

Once I got so excited that I sold our refrigerator. People were coming by and buying so many things that I stopped thinking clearly. I didn't like our refrigerator, anyway, and we were selling so many items and bringing in a lot of money . . . well, when someone asked what else I had for sale, I said, "How about the refrigerator?" It sold immediately. I was thrilled until Bob got home and heard the news. Let's just say I learned a good lesson.

Organization

Display sale items in categories. All the toys should go in one place, glassware and kitchen utensils in another, and so forth. Use tables—picnic tables and card tables are good—to display breakable items. You might want to cover the table tops with butcher paper or old tablecloths to give a tidy appearance.

Have an extension cord available from a garage or house outlet so people can check any electrical appliances such as popcorn popper, iron, razor, or clock. If the item doesn't work, tell the truth. Your interested customer may still buy it. Many garage-sale shoppers are handymen who can fix anything or salvage usable parts. Never underestimate what will sell. Don't say, "That's junk" and trash it. There are many creative people who will buy your "junk."

Cover not-for-sale items with old sheets or tarps. People will buy everything in the garage if you're not careful. You may need to make a few NOT FOR SALE signs, especially if the children's bikes are in open view.

Hospitality adds to the garage sale. Try serving hot coffee, tea, or ice tea. This is particularly nice during the first couple of hours in the morning.

Set Your Price

Pricing takes some time and thought. As a general rule, keep the prices down. Never mark directly on the article. If husband's shirt doesn't sell, he may go to the office one day with "$1.50" inked on the cuff or pocket. Stick-on labels, round stickers, or masking tape work best.

If individual family members are going to keep the money from the sale of certain items, be sure to mark those items with appropriate initials or color code. (Linda's the blue label, Tom's green, Krista's yellow, Erik's red.)

I like to price everything in fifty-cent increments. That gives you some bargaining power. Even with your low prices, people love to try and bring the price a little lower.

You might have separate boxes with items priced 5 cents, 10 cents, and 25 cents. This will save you from having to mark each individual item. You might even have a box marked FREE. Children love these boxes because they can shop while Mom and Dad look around.

Have one person, preferably an adult, be the cashier. All purchases go through that person. On a large sheet of poster board, list each person who is selling at your sale. As each item is sold, remove the price sticker and place it under his or her name, or write the price in the appropriate column. At the end of the day, just add each column and you're ready to divide the spoils.

By the way, it's best to accept only cash from your customers. Checks are okay if you know the person, but don't feel obligated. You don't have the advantage of a store that can match check numbers against a list of those whose checks have bounced.

Make Time Count

On the day of the sale, get up early and commit the day to the sale. We've found that people who know antiques and other valuable items hit the garage sales early, often the day before or an hour before you open. So be prepared and have everything set up the day before. When it's time, simply move the tables and other items outside onto the walkway, patio, or driveway.

Eat a good breakfast. You'll need a clear mind for bargain decisions. And pack lunches for you and your children the night before. You won't have time to make lunch when people are in your yard all day.

When you're done, keep in the festive mood and plan something special like a barbecue or have dinner out with some of the proceeds. It will put an appropriate finish on a wonderful day.

What do you do with the items that don't sell? The one thing you *don't* want to do is bring them back into your home. Remember, these are items you no longer use, need, or want. So place all the unsold items in bags or boxes and call an organization such as Salvation Army or Goodwill. They'll usually come and pick up the items. Be sure to get a receipt for a tax deduction.

Finally, don't forget to remove the signs you put up around the neighborhood to draw all those customers. It's best to do this as soon as the sale is over, or at latest, first thing the next morning.

Block Garage Sales

Many neighborhoods plan an annual garage sale involving several families on one street. This is an exciting tradition that draws a lot of interest in the participants as well as bargain hunters.

The organizational principles are the same. It involves at least one joint planning meeting so all the details can be discussed. Review all the particulars so the day runs smoothly.

You might want to appoint a committee to design and place the ad in the local newspaper announcing the sale. Be sure to emphasize that it is a *neighborhood* garage sale. That will draw a lot more interest from the shoppers. A joint sign-making committee will also save time and duplication of work.

It is very important that all families are ready when the sale starts.

An enjoyable end-of-day activity is to have a joint barbecue for all the participants. This builds neighborhood spirit and breaks down barriers you might have. Some neighborhoods have even had the local police department barricade off the block so the party can be held in the street. It's a lot of fun and a different way to have a party.

Ready to have a sale? Exhibit W is a checklist to help you prepare.

'Garage Sale' Checklist

ASSIGNMENT	DONE	COMMENT
1. Need for garage sale has been established.	✓	May 31st
2. Date has been set.	✓	May 31st
3. Ad has been placed in local newspaper.		Monday before sale.
4. Signs are made.	✓	
5. Signs are posted.		Evening before sale.
6. Signs are removed after garage sale.		
7. Garage is cleaned out. A. Child #1—Bedroom cleaned out B. Child #2—Bedroom cleaned out C. Child #3—Bedroom cleaned out D. _____ E. _____		The Saturday before sale.
8. Items for sale are assembled in one section of the garage or patio.		To be completed Wednesday before.
9. Display tables are identified.	✓	

EXHIBIT W

ASSIGNMENT	DONE	COMMENT

10. Day before sale:
  A. Price all items
  B. Set up tables
  C. Display items in categories
  D. Plug in extension cord (testing of appliances)
  E. Cover non-sale items with sheets or tarps
  F Make your large display board to keep track of individual sales account
  G. Make lunch for tomorrow
  H. Other _____
     _____
     _____
		To do on Friday.

11. Day of sale:
  A. Wake up early
  B. Post signs
  C. Move tables out of garage to sidewalks
  D. Coffee/tea is a nice gesture for the shoppers
  E. Have an adult or older child handle the "money box"
  F. As item is sold, credit the "account chart" under proper seller's name (see Account Chart)
		To be done Saturday.

ASSIGNMENT	DONE	COMMENT
G. Have a "quiet and gentle spirit"		
H. Place all the remaining items in bags or boxes. Call Salvation Army or Goodwill to come and pick up. Obtain receipt for tax deduction.		
I. Clean up		
J. Remove signs from neighborhood		
K. Clean up with a bath or shower		
L. Plan to have a barbecue (or maybe even dinner out)		*Hamburger Fry.*
M. Divide the profits for the day		
N. Evaluate the day		

Account Chart

DAD	MOM	BRAD	CRAIG	JENNY	CHRIS	CHAD
1.50	.50	.25	.50	2.00	.50	1.00
.75	1.00	1.00	2.50	1.50	1.00	.50
1.00	.50	1.50	1.00	.50	1.00	.50
						1.50
Totals:						
3.25	2.00	2.75	4.00	4.00	2.50	3.50

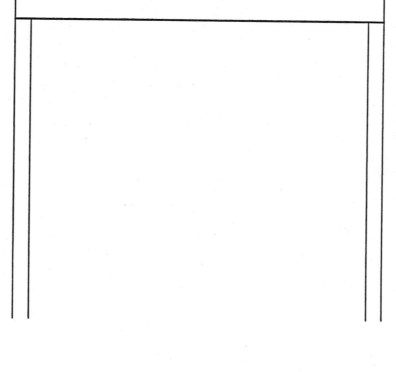

Part V

Survival Through Organized Vacations and Travel

Chapter 21

Organizing a Memorable Vacation

*A*s a child who grew up with a single parent, I never experienced summer vacations. I have no memories of travel or special family activities in new, exotic places. So with my husband and children it was hard, at first, for me to learn how to relax and enjoy our vacation trips. In fact, we spent several summer vacations at Forest Home Christian Conference Center in southern California. There are many similar camps throughout the United States that provide great spiritual teaching, food, entertainment, and fun for every member of the family. It's a balanced vacation with a purpose, all pre-planned for you.

I needed that kind of structure for a while. But I also began to realize that we could organize our own family fun. We could fly a kite over the Grand Canyon or ride bikes over the Golden Gate Bridge in San Francisco or roller-skate in New York City. We could meet new friends while camping, waterskiing, and beachcombing.

However, vacations don't just happen. When traveling with children on land, sea, or air, it is vital to think ahead to prevent "disaster" experiences. If we don't, even short trips can leave the whole family exhausted and in need of a *real* vacation.

Plan as a Family

Vacations are best planned by the entire family, including the children. Some evening after dinner, have a brainstorming session. Allow everyone to be creative and suggest people, places, and things they want to see and experience. Don't limit your ideas. Think of activities that will allow every family member to experience and learn something new. Perhaps some of your ideas may not be practical for this year or in the immediate future. But it is fun to dream, and you never know ... with all these great ideas in mind, maybe that once-in-a-lifetime dream vacation can be fulfilled.

On another evening, take some time to communicate your family vacation needs for the coming summer. Allow each family member to express his or her desire. Does one person want total rest? Another beautiful scenery? Water sports? Hiking or mountain climbing? All of the above? A balance of rest and activity?

Now we've got a list of needs and a list of potential vacations. The fun is in trying to see how we can match each person's needs with one or more vacation ideas. The more the children can participate, the better. Let them help on researching, looking at maps, planning the itinerary. If the children help plan the vacation, there will be less complaints like, "How long till we get there?" or "Do we have to do this?"

Plan Ahead

Once you've decided on the area(s) you want to visit,

gather as much information as you can about that area. Remember to find out the negatives as well as the positives so you can avoid potential problems.

• Write or call the Chamber of Commerce or a visitor/ tourist bureau in the area you plan to visit for literature giving specific recommendations for family vacations.

• Contact your auto club or travel agent for maps and information about the area you plan to cover.

• Talk with friends or people who have been where you plan to visit.

• Use the checklists in Exhibits X and Y to help you remember all the details.

Reservations and Arrangements

Make advance reservations at campgrounds, motels, and special tourist attractions as needed. Auto club and travel agents can alert you as to where you need reservations.

• Make sure you have written confirmation of your reservations, and carry them with you as you travel.

• If you're going to be late at a lodging or campsite, you can often guarantee your reservation by prepayment of the first night's stay.

• If you must cancel a reservation, do so as early as possible so you can get total refunds and allow others to take your place. A 48-hour notice will usually ensure you total refunds.

• When making reservations, check on lodging policies to see if children can sleep in parents' room at no extra charge.

• If you need a crib, reserve one at the time you make the reservation.

TRAVEL & VACATION CHECK LIST

Destination: _____

_____

Airlines: _____ Flight #: _____
Depart/Date & Time: _____
Arrival/Date & Time: _____
Airlines: _____ Flight #: _____
Depart/Date & Time: _____
Arrival/Date & Time: _____
Airlines: _____ Flight #: _____
Depart/Date & Time: _____
Arrival/Date & Time: _____

_____

Accommodations: _____
    Address: _____
    Phone: _____
    Children: _____

_____

    Pets: _____
Deliveries To Be Stopped: _____

_____

Mail: _____

_____

Special Purchases For Trip: _____

_____

Recommended Activities: _____

_____

Recommended Restaurants: _____

_____

Notes: _____

_____

_____

_____

EXHIBIT X

TRAVEL & VACATION PACKING LIST

Clothing
- [ ] Belts
- [ ] Blouses
- [ ] Boots
- [ ] Bras
- [ ] Coats
- [ ] Dresses
- [ ] Gloves
- [ ] Gowns
- [ ] Handkerchiefs
- [ ] Hats
- [ ] Jackets
- [ ] Jeans
- [ ] Jewelry
- [ ] Nightgowns
- [ ] Pajamas
- [ ] Pantyhose
- [ ] Raincoat
- [ ] Robes
- [ ] Scarves
- [ ] Shirts
- [ ] Shoes
- [ ] Skirts
- [ ] Slacks
- [ ] Slippers
- [ ] Slips
- [ ] Socks
- [ ] Suits
- [ ] Sweaters
- [ ] Swimsuits
- [ ] Ties
- [ ] Underwear

Toiletries & Grooming Aids
- [ ] Aftershave
- [ ] Body Creams & Lotions
- [ ] Comb
- [ ] Cotton Balls
- [ ] Dental Floss
- [ ] Deodorant
- [ ] Electric Shaver

- [ ] Face Creams & Lotions
- [ ] Hair Brush
- [ ] Hair Clips/Pins
- [ ] Hair Conditioner
- [ ] Hair Dryer
- [ ] Hair Rollers
- [ ] Hair Spray
- [ ] Magnifying Mirror
- [ ] Makeup
- [ ] Manicure Items
- [ ] Mouthwash
- [ ] Nail Brush
- [ ] Perfume/Cologne
- [ ] Razor Blades
- [ ] Shampoo/Rinse
- [ ] Shower Cap
- [ ] Soap/Soap Dish
- [ ] Sunburn Preventive
- [ ] Talc
- [ ] Toothbrush
- [ ] Toothpaste
- [ ] Tweezers

Medications & Health Aids
- [ ] Prescription Medication
- [ ] Bandages
- [ ] Antihistamine
- [ ] Birth Control
- [ ] Calamine Lotion
- [ ] Cotton-tipped Swabs
- [ ] Diarrhea Medicine
- [ ] Electric Heating Pad
- [ ] Eye Drops
- [ ] Foot Powder
- [ ] Indigestion Remedy
- [ ] Insect Repellent

- [ ] Laxative
- [ ] Motion Sickness Remedy
- [ ] Nasal Spray
- [ ] Pain Reliever
- [ ] Rubbing Alcohol
- [ ] Sanitary Napkins
- [ ] Sleeping Pills
- [ ] Thermometer
- [ ] Tranquilizers
- [ ] Vitamins

Miscellaneous
- [ ] Address Book
- [ ] Alarm Clock
- [ ] Batteries
- [ ] Briefcase
- [ ] Calculator
- [ ] Camera/Film
- [ ] Cash
- [ ] Checkbook
- [ ] Credit Cards
- [ ] Detergent/Iron
- [ ] Electric Converter
- [ ] Flashlight
- [ ] Gifts
- [ ] Hangers
- [ ] Luggage Tags
- [ ] Passport/Visas
- [ ] Pens/Pencils
- [ ] Playing Cards
- [ ] Radio
- [ ] Reading Material
- [ ] Safety Pins
- [ ] Scissors
- [ ] Sewing Kit
- [ ] Stamps
- [ ] Sunglasses
- [ ] Tape Recorder
- [ ] Travel Tickets
- [ ] Traveler's Checks
- [ ] Umbrella
- [ ] Wallet

• When driving, begin your trip early in the morning so that you can arrive in time for everyone to relax, take a swim, or enjoy a short walk. Allow for unexpected stops along the way to enjoy historical landmarks and spectacular views.

Finances

• Many hotels and restaurants will not accept out-of-town personal checks. So take a combination of credit cards, traveler's checks, or cash.

• Don't carry a lot of cash. What cash you do carry should be divided between husband and wife.

• Gasoline credit cards help reduce the amount of cash needed.

Car Organization

Here are a few more ideas that will help lessen the possibility of "Oops, I forgot the . . ." Remember to take the following as fits your needs:

• Child's favorite blanket for napping.

• A pillow.

• Towels to cover car seats and steering wheel in hot areas. They can also be used as pillows or to mop up spills.

• First-aid kit. Fill an empty coffee can with bandages, aspirin, antiseptic, thermometer, scissors, safety pins, tweezers, adhesive tape, gauze, cotton balls, and cotton swabs.

• A flashlight that works. Check the batteries before you leave home.

• A cloth drawstring bag (you can make one of these in a few minutes with some fabric scraps) to carry in the glove compartment or hang on a knob. This bag can contain such items as Handy Wipes or a damp washcloth in a plastic bag, "clean" snacks such as peanuts or gum, a daily devotional booklet, medium-sized plastic bags (children can use them for collectibles), a baby bib, and other miscellaneous items.

• Another bag can be hung on the back of the front seat or a car door to store play things for the children. This bag could contain crayons, scissors, glue, jump rope (for gas and rest stops), and games.

• A thermos of drinking water and paper cups. Or use a squirt bottle so the children can just squirt water into their mouths or each other's mouths.

• Bathing suits should be easily accessible, even on winter trips. Many hotels have hot tubs or heated pools.

• A camera to record your memories. It's great if you have an inexpensive camera that each child can use to take a few photos. That way he can make his own personal vacation scrapbook.

On the Road

• Picnic whenever possible. It's less expensive than fast-food stops and restaurants, and probably more nutritious.

• Remember, even baby needs a change of space and fresh air. Stop for a quick walk with the baby, or unfold the stroller and take a short, brisk walk. For driver safety and children's sanity, some sort of stop should be made every two hours.

• Depending on the age of your children, give them their own map so they can follow the route and tell you how far it is to the next town or stop.

• Provide pad and pencil for each child so he can keep a journal of the trip. Crayons are good, too, for illustrating what they see and do.

• One way to maintain order in the car is to give each child a bag filled with pennies, nickels, or dimes at the start of the vacation. Mom and Dad begin the vacation with an empty bag (no, not an empty wallet!). Each time a child is disobedient or naughty in some way, he must give up a coin from his bag and put it in the parent's bag. Any money the children have at the end of the trip is theirs to keep.

One last thing. Always take along a sense of humor! You can count on something going wrong. If you can laugh a little, it will help ease the tension.

After the vacation, plan a "remember when" evening. Review the movies, photos, scrapbooks, and journal. If the grandparents or friends are coming over, have each family member prepare to show and tell his or her favorite part of the trip. The memories are an important part of a vacation. I hope your family will have many wonderful memories.

Chapter 22

Travel Smart— Automobile Organization

"I sought the Lord, and He answered me, and delivered me from all my fears."

PSALM 34:4 NASB

So many women today are responsible for their own cars. To maximize our safety, I've prepared a checklist of practical items to keep in the car, plus a few things to do to prevent or minimize problems. You can't be too careful in this area, so travel smart.

Here are the things you should keep in your glove compartment:

- Maps
- Notepad and pen
- Tire pressure gauge
- Handy Wipes
- Sunglasses
- Mirror (this can be kept above the sun visor)
- Extra pair of nylon hose for that unexpected run
- Reading material—especially a pocket-size Bible so you can enjoy prayer and Bible reading during waiting times in the car

- Can opener
- Plastic fork and spoon
- Change for phone calls (or tolls if you live in certain parts of the country)
- Business cards
- Band-Aids
- Matches
- Stationery—again, waiting can be used constructively to catch up on correspondence
- Scissors, nail clippers
- Children's books and/or games

And here are a few more things to keep in your trunk. Many of them can be put in a shoebox and stored neatly in the trunk. Or a plastic dishpan serves well and can also be used to carry water in an emergency:

- Authorized empty gas can
- Fuses
- Jumper cables
- Flares
- Screwdriver
- Extra fan belt and spark plugs
- Flashlight (check the batteries periodically)
- First-aid kit
- Fire extinguisher—there are small ones made especially for automobiles
- Instructions on how to change a tire
- Blanket/towel
- Chains—for winter months
- Snow scraper
- Rope

Protect Your Car

• Hide a key in case you ever lock your keys inside the car. (Caution: Don't put the key under the hood if you have an inside hood release.)

• Print your name, address, and phone number on a 3″ x 5″ card (or use your business card) and slide it down your car window frame on the driver's side. If your car is ever lost or stolen, this will help you prove the auto is yours.

• If you live in a potentially snowy area, keep a bag of kitty litter in your trunk. This will help you get traction if you're ever stuck in snow.

• Your rubber car mats can be used to prevent your windshield from freezing. Put them on the outside of the windows and use the wipers to hold them in place. If there's snow or ice, you won't have to scrape.

• Your car may not start if your battery terminals become corroded. Simply scrub them with a mixture of one cup baking soda and two cups water. It cleans them right up!

• You might want to have a rechargeable, battery-run hand vacuum to keep the car interior clean.

• If you aren't mechanically inclined, then you'd be wise to find a qualified mechanic you can trust, preferably one who has developed a good reputation. Keep your car well-serviced. Follow your maintenance manual for regular oil changes and tune-ups. Check the tires every 5,000 miles to make sure the tread is not wearing low.

A car, like our homes, reflects who we are. A well-maintained, organized, and clean (inside and out) automobile can reduce a lot of stress in our lives. It doesn't take long each week to maintain our cars. And we will benefit in the long run when we trade it in or sell it.

Chapter 23

Travel for Less

"So teach us to
number our days,
that we may present
to Thee a heart of
wisdom."

PSALM 90:12 NASB

I read once that on a typical airplane there were up to 37 different prices paid to get to the same destination. The wise shopper becomes aware of how to travel for less, regardless of the mode of travel.

Money saved in travel can help you meet other budgetary items, and can even drop to the bottom line as increased savings.

Whether you travel by plane or by car, you can cut costs as you go.

Fly for Less

• Select a very competent travel agent near your home. Build a relationship with that person so he or she becomes very familiar with your travel needs. I try not to spread my business around to various agents because I want my agent to know of my loyalty concerning my flying needs.

• Enroll in each of the various airline "mileage plus" programs. I also narrow my business to one or two different airlines so these miles accumulate faster.

225

• Ask for senior-citizen discount rates if you qualify.

• Ask your travel agent for the most economical flights. Then check other airlines yourself to make sure you really are getting the best price. (Larger city newspapers usually have a comparison chart between various cities.)

• Be willing to travel at off-peak times and at night, when prices are lower.

• Try to make your reservations at least 21 days before departure, and if at all possible plan to stay over at least one Saturday. (This is a huge savings.)

• Talk to friends who have traveled to your destination. They can give you suggestions that can be cost savers.

• Look in the travel section of your local paper for special rates.

• Be careful in selecting unknown businesses. If a rate sounds too good to be true, it probably is.

• You can save money by flying into a hub city like Chicago, Dallas, Denver, or Atlanta and making a connecting flight. One stop and straight-through flights will cost you more money.

Automobile Saving Tips

• Plan ahead. When you go on vacation, plan to travel during the workweek to avoid weekend traffic. This is particularly true during summer and main holiday periods.

• When traveling through large cities, note the peak freeway travel times for the commuters. It might be cost- and time-efficient to bypass larger cities during peak travel times.

• Remember to accelerate gently.

• Watch traffic ahead in order to anticipate or avoid stops. It is cost-efficient to coast up to traffic and gently accelerate, rather than racing to traffic, coming to a dead stop, then accelerating to full speed.

• Maintain proper speed limits. Going too slow and too fast burns your fuel much faster than abiding by the 30–65 mph limits throughout America. It takes 30 percent more gas to travel at 70 mph than 50 mph.

• Snow tires reduce mileage by one to three miles per gallon, so don't put them on too soon and don't keep them on any longer than necessary.

• Keep your car properly serviced. A well-maintained car will be cheaper to operate, easier to handle, and give you longer wear than a poorly serviced car. It will also bring more value when you are ready to sell or trade it in for another one.

• To save more gas, don't just use the correct tire pressure, which is usually listed on a sticker pasted to the driver's door, but add four to five pounds more per square inch (psi), as long as you don't exceed 32 psi. This will also increase the life of your tires. Check your air pressure once a week.

• Drive moderately on long grades or when climbing steep hills. Pressing the accelerator pedal all the way down only wastes gas.

• Be sensitive when using your air conditioning and electrical accessories like radio, lighters, bright lights, and rear window defrosters. The power which activates and runs these comes from motors which are driven by elements which reduce gas mileage.

• Don't "top off" your gas tank. Spilled gas costs you money.

• You can get better gas mileage (15 percent more) by maintaining your car properly. Tune the engine, adjust the wheel alignment, use the proper multiweight motor oil, and have proper tire pressure.

• Take your car to a trusted mechanic for a thorough check before each long trip. Be sure that all belts are checked for proper tension and wear.

• If at all possible, don't use roof racks. The added wind resistance will cause a tremendous drop in fuel efficiency. If you must have a roof rack, make a wedge out of your containers toward the front and place the larger items to the rear. Make sure you have the boxes well secured so that the rack won't fall off in travel. At each of your stops along the way you would be wise to check the strapping.

• Use your cruise control setting when driving a long distance. Maintaining steady speed in freeway driving will give you increased gas mileage.

• Keep windows closed at highway speeds. Open windows create aerodynamic drag, which increases fuel consumption.

• Don't let your car idle for long periods of time. An idling engine wastes about a quart of gas every 15 minutes.

• Don't warm up your car's engine by letting it idle. Start it up and drive right off slowly. The engine warms up faster when driving than it does when idling.

• Revving the engine before shutting it off not only wastes fuel but also leaves raw gasoline in the cylinders which then leaks down and dilutes the motor oil.

Once you become aware that you can save in your travels, you and your family will have a creative time in figuring out how you can save. Then what are you going to do with the money you save?

Chapter 24

Family Cruises Can Be Fun

"For by me your days will be multiplied, and years of life will be added to you."

PROVERBS 9:11 NASB

*O*n both our twenty-fifth and thirty-fifth wedding anniversaries, Bob and I have taken cruises to celebrate these memorable milestones in our marriage. The first one was along the coast of Mexico and the second one was touring the Caribbean Islands. What fun and adventure! They came well past our children going with us, but we were exposed to several couples who did bring their young children along. At first I wasn't convinced that this might be a good idea. But after watching these interactions for a week, we soon changed our minds. Now we encourage families in that age group to seriously give it a thought.

Since then, I have rarely met a family that hasn't enjoyed a cruise. The ship serves as a floating resort that takes you to a new and exciting place each day. And yet it works especially well for families because you and your children know the restaurant and the ship environment. It's such a comfortable, familiar place to return to every evening. This daily potpourri of different ports and islands gives you and your family a sample of what that particular location has to offer. Since our initial tours, we are determined to go back again for a more in-depth visit to a specific location.

Nothing beats the luxury of sitting on a deck chair for two hours knowing that your children are happily, safely involved nearby. It's a no-brainer vacation—that's the beauty of it. Once you've made the reservations (and, of course, paid for the trip), all you have to do is show up and the cruise leaders take over. You determine how much you do or do not want to do.

In my observations and discussions with many families who have experienced this adventure, there are several suggestions they make. Use the planning time as a teaching time. The whole family can become involved in familiarizing themselves with the geography of the regions to be visited. You can talk about time differences, different time zones, travel time, and mileage calculations (both of plane, train, or car to get to the departure dock, and also the mileage traveled on board ship). What about differences in climate, temperature, clothes, food, and color of skin?

You can go through the guides and make a plan for each day's activities. What points of interest do you want to visit? Does everyone want to go or would some family members just as soon stay on board ship and relax? (Small children are not always able to keep up with a hectic tour schedule.) Ships have necessary personnel to babysit with all ages of children. There are many daily activities planned on board ship for those who want to stay aboard. Before you select a cruise line, be sure to check out their offerings. Some ships are geared for families and some aren't. Ask questions!

Even get your family involved in setting up a basic budget for the trip. The children will have a greater appreciation for this type of vacation when they are involved in planning the costs. They also can be in on the decision process if certain activities aren't available because of monetary limitations.

You don't have to be overly protective about your children's safety. The cruise line has taken a lot of protective precautions to prevent any accidents. There is protective netting around the deck, and all ship personnel are alerted to watch the young ones.

Even sharing the same cabin with the children isn't as bad as it might sound. It turns out that you hardly see them except when you want or at the end of the day. Set a routine time to meet at the cabin and talk about what you as a family have done all day, dress for dinner, and maybe even look over tomorrow's plans and activities. This time together will really be a terrific family time.

These cruises have one great advantage, and that is you can give your children an enormous amount of freedom. Once they know your cabin number, you can basically let them roam on their own. Cabin stewards are always available to help children when necessary, and it gives them a great feeling of autonomy and independence.

If you have a toddler, be aware that lots of cruise ships don't have bathtubs except in very expensive accommodations. So be sure to introduce your child to showers *before* you take the cruise.

Many parents with older children stress the importance of the whole family attending the first night orientation for adults and children. Do whatever you have to do to drag your kids to that meeting. They'll see what the universe of the ship is all about, and they'll find out what's available and what isn't. They'll also meet the other kids on the cruise. Instantly they probably will meet someone they like and are virtually inseparable thereafter.

If you want to explore on shore as a family, it may be cheaper to hire your own car and driver than to take the ship's planned excursions. You can make arrangements in advance, or ship personnel can make the arrangements for you during the cruise. If you are not sure about

232 • Emilie Barnes

local restaurants, have your cabin steward pack a lunch for you.

Teenagers love cruise ships. Parents never have to ask where they are going and never have to pass out all those restrictions that can make family vacations such a hassle. Many cruise lines have some especially good teen programs. Remember: "Ask the questions!"

One of the biggest attractions on a family cruise vacation is the food. Without a doubt you have never seen so much variety, color, flavor, and exotic food presentations. If you know the word "abundance," this will certainly make you aware of overabundance. This will give you, as parents, a great opportunity to practice your family manners. You would do well to start out about two weeks ahead of the cruise to talk about manners, proper conduct, and proper dress (particularly for the evening meals, which are dressy). Breakfast, lunch, and midnight buffets are usually more casual in attire. What a wonderful diversity of food! Each family member will have to make food choices that they have never had to make before. Waste is easy if we don't make responsible decisions. The ship personnel are great at the meals. They are usually from a different country, so this experience will be a great learning opportunity for you and the children.

If you are interested in this type of travel, contact "Travel with Your Children" and request their comprehensive booklet called "Cruising with Children." To order a copy, contact the organization at 45 West 18th Street, 7th Floor Tower, New York, NY 10011. Telephone: (212) 206-0688. The cost is $20.

Happy Cruising!

Part VI

Survival Through Organized Finances

Record-Keeping Made Simple

*T*his is the year to get our records, bills, and receipts out of shoeboxes, closets, drawers, and old envelopes. I found that I could clean out my wardrobe closet fairly easily. An old skirt, a stained blouse, or a misfit jacket I had little difficulty tossing. However, where and when I should toss old financial records was very difficult. I didn't want to do the wrong thing, so I kept—usually too long.

At income tax time, my neck always got stiff because I knew Bob was going to ask for a canceled check or a paid invoice, and I wasn't sure if I had it or not. At that point I made a decision to get my record-keeping in order so that it was a very easy process to keep my records up-to-date.

I sat down and looked at the whole process of record-keeping and began to break it down into logical steps. My first step was to decide to keep my records. Since I like things to be in order with the minimum amount of paperwork, I had a tendency to throw away records that should have been saved. I found that throwing away Bob's salary stubs, last year's tax return, and current receipts for medical or business expenses would only bring problems further down the road.

Our CPA says that throwing away financial records is the biggest mistake that people make. Throwing away records that later turn out to be important causes people a lot of unnecessary work and worry, he cautioned. When you have an IRS audit and you can't prove your deductions by a canceled check or a paid invoice, you will lose that deduction for the year, plus be subject to a fine and interest. Records are very important.

Good financial records help you make decisions very quickly. In just a few moments you can retrieve valuable information so that a decision can be made for budget planning, future purchases, or just anticipated future income.

As I began to develop a plan in which to establish good record-keeping, I came up with a seven-step plan.

Step 1: Know what to keep. I discovered that records generally fall into two categories: *permanent* records (important to keep throughout your life) and *transitory* records (dealing with your current circumstances).

Permanent records would include personal documents required in applying for credit, qualifying for a job, or proving entitlement to Social Security and other government programs. Birth and marriage certificates, Social Security cards, property records, college transcripts, diplomas, and licenses fall into this category.

Deciding how long to retain transitory records can be more difficult because often you don't know how long you'll need them. As a rule of thumb I suggest you keep all employment records until you leave the job. Other transitory records you want to keep include receipts for any major purchases you have made: jewelry, autos, art, and stock certificates, as well as tax returns and receipts for at least three years, health insurance policies, credit union membership, and company stock ownership plans.

Canceled checks not relating directly to specifics like home improvements should be kept for a minimum of three years in case of a tax audit. However, I will usually keep them for five to six years just to make sure I'm not throwing any records away that I might need on a tax audit.

If you own your home, apartment, or mobile home, be sure to retain the receipts for any improvements you make until you sell the property. They become proof that you added to the property's value and reduce any capital gains you might owe. Don't discard these receipts or tax returns from the years in which you paid for the improvements. I usually make a copy of these kind of receipts and keep a permanent copy in my "Home" folder. I have found that this saves a lot of valuable time when I need to justify each record. In my "Home" folder I also keep a running log with date, improvement made, cost, and receipt for each expenditure. At any given time we know how much money we have invested in our home. This information really helps when you get ready to sell your home and want to establish a sales price.

Your tax return, wage statements, and other papers supporting your income and deductions should be kept at least three years (that's the IRS statute of limitations for examining your return). I retain our records for seven years because the IRS has the right to audit within seven years if they believe you omitted an item accounting for more than 25 percent of your reported income, or indefinitely if they believe you committed fraud.

Step 2: Know yourself when you set up your system. Try to keep your system as simple as you can. I have found that the more disorganized you are, the simpler the system should be. It doesn't make sense to set up an elaborate filing system if it is too complicated for you to follow.

I suggest that you consider these points when setting up your system:

• How much time can you devote to record-keeping? The less time you have, the simpler your system should be.

• Do you like working with numbers? Are you good at math? If so, your system can be more complex.

• How familiar are you with tax deductions and financial planning? If you are a beginner, set up a simple system.

• Will anyone else be contributing records to the system?

This last point is a very important consideration if you are married. Usually our mate will have a different opinion on what type of system we will have. I have found among married couples it's best to determine who is most gifted in this area and let that person take care of the records. Bob and I get along very well in this area. I write the checks for our home expenses and balance this account's checking statement. Then I forward everything to Bob for record-keeping. In our family he is the most gifted in this area of our life.

We have found that the simplest way to organize receipts for tax purposes is to keep two file folders: one for deduction items and another for questionable items. At tax time all you have to do is total up each category and fill in the blank. Be sure to double-check the other entries for overlooked possibilities.

If your return is more complex, set up a system with individual folders for the various deductions you claim: medical and dental expenses, business, travel and entertainment, property taxes, mortgage interest, child-care services. When you pay a bill, drop the receipt into the right folder. At the end of the year you'll be able to tally the receipts and enter the totals on your tax forms.

Be sure to take your questionable deduction folder with you when you go to see your CPA. Go over each item to see if it is eligible for a deduction. As you can tell by reading this chapter, I strongly endorse using a professional tax preparer. Our tax returns have become difficult and the tax laws so complex that good stewardship of our monies is to go to a professional. Professionals will save you much more than you will spend for their services.

Your checkbook can be your best record-keeper if you check off entries that might count as tax deductions. If you have a personal computer at home, you have a wide selection of software programs to help you keep track of these records.

Step 3: Set aside a spot for your records. Generally, home rather than office is the best place for personal documents. A fireproof, waterproof file cabinet or desk drawer will do for transitory records. However, I use and have thousands of other ladies all across the United States using our "perfect boxes" for storage of records. See my chapter "From Total Mess to Total Rest" for more details regarding the use of these boxes.

Permanent documents generally should be kept in a safe-deposit box. However, a will and important final instructions should be kept elsewhere because, in many states, safe-deposit boxes are sealed following the owner's death, even if someone else has a key.

Step 4: Tell someone where your records are. As I travel around the country conducting seminars, many of the ladies share with me they don't know where their husbands have vital information written down, sharing who to contact in case of death. None of us think about death because it is so far away, but we must share this important information with someone who will need to know.

Each year Bob reviews with me his "data sheet" listing all the information regarding insurance policies, stock and investments, mortgage locations, banking account information, contents in safe-deposit boxes, etc. That information is very helpful and reassuring to me in case of any changes in our status.

Even if you're a whiz at keeping financial records, it's not much use if no one else knows where any of the records are located.

As a family, make up a list noting where your records are located and give it to a family member or trusted friend.

Step 5: Get professional advice on handling records. As I've shared previously in this chapter, Bob and I recommend you seek professional advice on how better records can translate into tax savings in the future. The expense is well worth the investment of time and money. You can also go to your local bookstore and purchase any number of good paperback books on this topic. Be a reader and a learner. It will serve you well.

Step 6: Change your record-keeping system when you make a life change. Major life shifts—a job move, marriage, death, divorce, separation—signal a time to revamp your records. Starting a home-based business also means it's time to talk to a professional regarding new tax allowances. A life change does necessitate a change in record-keeping.

The costs of looking for a new job in the same field and a job-related move can mean you're eligible for a new tax deduction, so be sure to file all receipts.

Step 7: Set aside time for your record-keeping. Try to set a regular time each month to go over your financial records so that you won't be a wreck come April when you have to file your tax return. The best system in the world won't work if you don't use it or keep it current.

Many people prefer to update records when they pay bills. Others file receipts, update a ledger of expenses, and look over permanent records once a month when reconciling a checking account. Whatever works best for you is what's important. You should update at least once a month. If not, you will create a lot of stress as you play catch-up. The goal of simple record-keeping is to reduce stress in our lives, not to increase the stress.

I have found that time is worth money. When I can reduce time spent, I can increase money because my energy is better used on constructive efforts rather than dealing with emergencies and putting out fires.

Schedule a plan and plan a schedule

Chapter 26

Cheaper Can Be Better

"He who gathers money little by little makes it grow."
PROVERBS 13:11 NIV

We live in a day when we pay extra for our clothes, vacations, food, and cars if they have a certain name or logo insignia embossed on them. Never did I think that I would wear someone's name brand and give them a free billboard advertising their product. Just take a moment and think of the names that mean so much to you and your children. The Madison Avenue executives have certainly captured your children with proper names for their buying power. When it comes time to buy clothes for your children, you need to know the right brand of athletic shoes, socks, trousers, shirts, blouses, shampoo, hair spray, etc. The list can go on and on. We are slaves of the advertising industry.

Bob and I have a couple of mottos which we remember when exercising our buying power. They are "Less Is Best" and "Cheaper Can Be Better."

In our youth we wanted to accumulate things. Wherever we went we shopped for new things: sofas, pictures, carpets, drapes, beds, televisions, record players (before cassettes and compact discs), crystal, china, silver, pewter, etc. As we have gotten older, we realize that all this stuff has to be taken care of by storage space, washing, dusting, repairs, and replacement. We have told our children, family, and friends that we don't want any more *stuff*. We only want consumable items—nothing that takes up shelf space, counter space, or needs dusting. This means that "Less Is Best" in our lives. That means no more bowls, platters, serving trays, silver teapots, crystal goblets, silver cake knives, or any of those items we used to think were so important. In fact, we are beginning to think that someday we will be selling some of our stuff. We are tired of taking care of all this stuff!

Our second motto is "Cheaper Can Be Better." Isn't this a new concept? Along with our fixation with proper labels and logos, we have been sold a bill of goods that says value is reflected by higher prices. In many cases this is true. Over the years I have learned that quality costs more. My mother used to always say, "You only get what you pay for." Since she was in the clothing business, she knew good fabrics by the very touch of her fingers. There are times when you can buy the quality goods through other means and make a wonderful savings. We have two wonderful stores in our community that have great clothes. When I walk in these stores on any given day, I can find an item of clothing I would love to purchase, but I've learned that if I wait until their sales occur (which is more often than they used to), I can save anywhere from 25–70 percent for the same item. It takes some discipline and delaying of gratification, but it shows that cheaper is better.

There are many examples that prove this old adage, "Cheaper Can Be Better."

Clothing Better for Less

- Wait for sales in your favorite department store.

• Locate factory outlets near your home in which to shop. Sometimes you have to drive an hour or more to shop, but the savings are worth the drive. Bunch up your desired purchases so you can buy several items at a time. Also let your friends and family know that you are going. See if they need anything while you are there. Who knows, they may even want to go with you!

• In larger cities many manufacturers have "seconds" outlets which give tremendous savings to the public. Examine the item carefully to make sure you can accept the flaw to the item. Many times the flaw won't show, or an inexpensive designer patch can go over the spot and give an added flair to the garment.

• In Southern California we have several stores which purchase seconds, over-runs, and year-end styles from leading manufacturers which they discount at great savings.

• Look for recycled clothing stores. Particularly in larger cities there are stores that take on consignment, secondhand items which have only been worn once or twice. Bob and I love to go into Pasadena and look at these recycled clothing stores. You would be amazed at the fashions and bargains.

• Let your friends, relatives, and business associates know that you would be interested in buying or trading for some of their clothes when they get tired of them. Our son, Brad, gives most of his older clothes to a high school principal in our area. Tom just loves to get Brad's clothes. They usually are like new. I have several friends who love to purchase my clothes. They are a perfect fit and style, and the price is right. Look and talk around. There are a lot of bargains in someone's closet. Start a co-op with other mothers and swap baby clothes. Save those clothes in a "perfect box" for storage of "First Year," "Second Year," "Third Year," etc. When either one of your younger children reach that age or a friend has a need for those clothes, you have a ready supply. What a bargain! Many of these are great for everyday wear, and if you're lucky you might even get some "special-wear" clothes.

Eating Better for Less

• Fruits and vegetables grown by local farmers tend to be fresher and more nourishing than those shipped from afar. My Bob has a wonderful home-grown garden, which is the best and cheapest. His garden provides us all year round with the best in fruits, vegetables, and flowers.

• Pasta sauces made entirely of tomatoes and other vegetables have less fat and fewer calories than meaty ones. Add chicken or turkey at home. These meats have less fat and are more inexpensive and more nutritious for your family.

• Get day-old pastries and breads. Bob just loves this bargain table in the market. You usually save 50 percent. These items are also good for making stuffing, French toast, and bread puddings.

• Ground chuck makes juicier, tastier hamburgers than ground round or ground sirloin. (You might be interested in my cookbooks that give you some healthier meat alternatives in your meal planning. See page 273 for information regarding ordering.)

• Canned light tuna is preferable for use in recipes to the more costly solid white; it's less dry and has a richer flavor.

• For stews, pot roasts, and other dishes that are cooked a long time, cheaper cuts of meat (such as chuck) tend to be more moist and flavorful. I highly recommend at my seminars the purchase of a crockpot for your kitchen.

Start your meal in the morning, and at dinnertime it's ready for you to sit down and enjoy. Just add a salad and some French bread, and your meal will be complete. When buying a crockpot, choose one that has the pot that can be lifted out for ease of cleaning. (Don't get the type that requires the pot to be cleaned together with the heating elements.)

• Bruised, overripe bananas from the bargain bin add a much stronger flavor to banana breads, muffins, ice cream, and fruit puree than firm, perfect fruit.

• Many frozen vegetables such as green peas and green beans are better and more nourishing than fresh ones because they're frozen within hours of picking.

• Choose whole-grain breads and cereals rather than refined ones. You'll get more fiber as well as B vitamins and minerals (try the day-old bin).

• Potatoes boiled or baked whole in their skins retain nearly all their vitamins and minerals. Halving or peeling causes nutrient loss.

• Change your meal pattern. Instead of the same old routine—meats, potatoes, and vegetables for dinner every day—serve a hearty soup, an unusual casserole, or a main-dish salad. Again, you might be interested in some of my cookbooks which are self-published. (See page 273 for ordering information.)

• Buy plain, unsweetened cereals and add sliced fruit, raisins, and/or nuts instead of sugar.

Take a hand calculator with you when you shop. Then you can break the cost down for true cost comparisons.

• Shop from a preselected list of foods from your menu planner. Through some preplanning of meals you can save $15 to $20 per week. Don't buy impulsively. Use discipline.

• Get in and out of the market as quickly as possible. The longer you stay, the more you will spend.

• Don't go food shopping when you are hungry because hungry people buy more.

• Try not to take your children shopping with you. They will put pressure on you to buy TV items. Your food costs will be higher. (As the children enter their teens, there is valuable teaching that can take place at the supermarket, but not when they are too young.)

• Don't assume that items at the end of aisles that are eye-catching are the cheapest or on sale. Look on lower shelves for other selections. Many times generic or other brands have good cost value.

• Get in the habit of using coupons. Be selective in buying only items you normally use. (However, venture out occasionally for an item you don't normally purchase. You might like your new brand better, and hopefully it will cost less.)

• Look behind newly marked, higher-priced items at the front of a shelf. You may find a few of them still marked at the old price. (However, many of the new cash registers have taken away this possibility. Still, look through.)

Getting More for Your Money at Home

• Toweling your hair and letting it dry naturally will leave it silkier and healthier than any hair dryer.

• Hand-washing is kinder than machine-washing to most sweaters, even wool.

• A personal note is warmer and more appreciated than the most elaborate card you can buy. (A great source for cost-savings stationery is Current Inc., The Current Building, Colorado Springs, CO 80941.)

• Large economy sizes of detergent and other household products create a lot less packaging waste to clog landfills than smaller sizes. (Purchase these bigger volumes with friends or neighbors, and divide the items up to reduce costs.)

• Mixed-breed pets from a shelter are usually better with kids and less illness-prone than purebred animals.

• A gift of time—whether to run errands, babysit, or simply listen—is often more valuable to the recipient than anything you can buy. Be creative and make a gift certificate out of your art supplies.

• For medical emergencies that are not life-threatening, you'll usually get faster, more personal care at a low-cost clinic than in a hospital emergency room.

• Plain cotton underwear is more absorbent and less apt to encourage bacteria than lacy lingeries. However, I do recommend lacy lingerie when you want to feel elegantly like a lady or for that special romantic weekend with your husband.

• A newsy letter, video recording, or audio cassette recording to a distant family member or friend may be far more appreciated than a long-distance call. After all, you can't reread or share a call.

• Cool houses are healthier than warm ones in winter, and each degree you lower your thermostat cuts fuel costs by about three percent. One of my observations in life has been that families which have a lot of sickness also have hot, dingy, and poorly ventilated homes. Open up the curtains, open a window or door, and let a breeze flow through your home. Don't let it get too warm or dark.

• Tums® antacid tablets are a more effective source of calcium than many costly calcium supplements. Check with your doctor before making the substitution.

• Laser discs produce higher quality pictures and sound than videotapes and they're cheaper to buy, though not as readily available to rent. This will be the next break-through in home entertainment for the 1990s.

• Turn the thermostat to its lowest setting if you won't be home for a few days. You can turn off the heating system completely if there's no danger of pipes freezing while you're away.

• Empty cardboard milk cartons make wonderful kindling for fires—so do candle stubs.

• To make newspaper logs, coat a three-foot dowel or a section of broomstick with paste wax. When the wax dries, buff it to a smooth finish. Place a newspaper on a large, flat surface. Hold the dowel firmly at each end and roll sheets of paper onto the dowel as tightly as you can. Tightly rolled logs burn much longer than loosely rolled ones. Continue to roll paper onto the dowel until the roll is three to three-and-one-half inches in diameter. Carefully holding the paper in place, fasten the log firmly at each end and in the center with wire. Slide the dowel out of the roll and repeat to make as many logs as needed.

Saving on the Road

• Walking or cycling short distances does more for your health and the environment than driving.

• Choosing canvas or nylon carry-on luggage over heavy molded suitcases will save you time, money, and lost-luggage hassles.

• Sharing rides with a friend makes long trips less tedious than driving alone. Try carpooling.

• Off-season rates at first-class resorts are lower than regular prices at second-rate places. Time your trips with the season rates. Usually you also have less crowds.

• Weekend specials at big-city hotels offer better values than standard rates at modest establishments. Many fine hotels also make breakfast part of the package at no extra charge. I recommend these packages for short mini-vacations for a couple. Get a babysitter and escape for a romantic weekend.

• Many small inns and private homes provide more comfortable accommodations at lower cost than large hotels.

• Try to make your plane reservations at least 21 days in advance and include a stay-over through Saturday. This will give you a great savings. If you are a senior citizen, ask for a possible discount. Many airlines give an additional ten percent discount. Car rental companies also offer preplanned reservations.

• Be on the lookout for newspaper advertisements announcing special deals. Many times it will include airline, hotel, and car rental.

• Be willing to travel at off-peak times and at night, when prices are lower.

Get in the habit of jotting down ideas on how you can purchase what you want and need by purchasing cheaper. After a while you won't ever want to buy items at regular prices again. Remember, money reflects labor. Every dollar saved reflects a fraction of your hourly rate on the job. Depending on your hourly rate, you may not be willing to pay an extra $10 to $20 if it reflects one to four hours of labor.

Yes, cheaper can be better. Start today and find it to be a true axiom.

Super Energy— Money-Saving Tips

s wise managers of your home, Bob and I continually look at ways we can be more cost efficient. We start with each month's utility bills to see if they are about normal. If they're below normal, we always beam a smile to each other. But if one is larger than normal, we begin to ask some basic questions:

1. Why is this item out of line (a change of seasons, fluctuation of temperature—hotter, colder, etc., lack of rain, or a change in rates)? We might even have a faulty appliance or a possible leakage of water or gas—or maybe leaving lights on longer than normal.

2. Was there an error in reading the meter? Call the utility company and ask for a new reading. The rate per usage could be wrong. The unit multiplication could be wrong, which would give an error in calculation.

3. How can we reduce or keep our energy costs down? Maybe we need to be more careful in our use

of these appliances. Bob and I used to get the whole family involved. This makes a great topic for "Family Conference Time" (see chapter 15).

Periodically, our local newspaper has a headline on "Rising Energy Costs." We read and hear this phrase all too often these days. No longer can any of us afford to be energy wasters, for the expense is just too great for all of us. In this chapter I have attempted to give you a few ideas to help you keep a handle on your energy costs. As you will see, it isn't a comprehensive list. You and the other members of your family will readily identify additional ways to conserve energy. Children love to be involved in this type of Sherlock Holmes work.

We spend needless money on heating and electric bills because we don't know the best ways to run our home and appliances. Here are some exciting tips to help you save lots of money by being aware of things to do to help cut down those high utility bills.

Lights Out

Did you know that it's cheaper to turn the lights off and on when entering and leaving a room than to leave them on (plus your light bulbs will last longer)?

Several lamps around our home have timers. Timers can be purchased in most hardware stores and will turn your lights on and off automatically. The savings could add up to 25 percent of your yearly electric bill. Plus it gives strangers the impression that someone is home while you are away.

Fluorescent lights use less electricity than regular light bulbs. They also illuminate more efficiently than incandescent bulbs. A 40-watt fluorescent tube gives more light than a 100-watt incandescent bulb while using less than half the current.

You may want to begin a "lights out" program in your home.

Dimmer switches can be purchased at most hardware stores and are very easily installed. These can increase your light bulb life up to 12 times and at the same time reduce your electricity usage.

• *One will do.* Rearrange your rooms. Let one properly shaded light do the work of three or four. If you're redecorating, use light colors. Dark colors absorb light.

• *Use lower watt bulbs.* Try three-way bulbs—they let you adjust lighting intensity for your needs.

• *Turn off all outdoor lights* . . . except those necessary for safety and security.

• *If you install bright security lights,* consider controlling them with a photoelectric cell or timer that turns the lights on at dusk and off at dawn so you can avoid burning the lights unnecessarily. Fairly new on the market are floodlights which are activated by motion. These are great for illuminating certain areas when a family member comes home after dark. The light stays on only when there is motion, then it turns off. This type of light is excellent for home security.

• *To monitor lights in remote areas of the house,* another possibility is to install a switch with a red pilot indicator on it. When the red light glows, you'll know lights in those areas have been left on. These remote switches are available at hardware stores.

• *Make sure that bulbs in remote places (attic, basement, garage, or closets) haven't been left burning* by installing automatic switches that shut off lights in a room when the door is closed.

• *It's better to use one large bulb* than several smaller ones. It requires six 25-watt bulbs to produce the light of a single 100-watt bulb.

• *It's important that light fixtures be kept clean,* because a dusty or dirty light fixture will absorb light and cause family members to turn on additional lights.

Heaters Can Work for You

• Should you have a gas-fired heating system, have it professionally cleaned and serviced at least once a year. The oil-fired systems should be cleaned and serviced at least two times a year.

• For any heating system (forced air, hot water, steam, electric) keep radiators, air registers, and ducts clean, clear of dirt and debris, and free of obstructions such as furniture and drapes.

• Some families install an electronic ignition on their gas furnace. This does away with the need for a continuously burning pilot light and increases your savings dramatically.

• You can save on heating costs by dressing to retain body heat. Layer extra clothes so that as the day warms up you can remove layers if you become too warm.

• A simple thing like keeping your windows sparkling clean in winter can help warm your home. Spotless window glass lets in more sunlight than grimy panes.

• To maintain your home's temperature, latch the windows instead of merely closing them. This gives a tighter seal.

• Install dual-glazed windows when building a new home or remodeling an older home. This can represent a savings of eight to ten percent on your utility bills.

• Make sure that the damper in your fireplace is closed when it isn't being used. The open chimney allows a lot of valuable heat to escape.

• Remove window screens before winter arrives because fine mist screen can reduce the amount of warming sunlight entering your home by up to 20 percent.

• Hot bathwater will help you keep your bathroom warm in cold-weather months if you allow the water to cool down before draining the tub. The water will add humidity that will also contribute to your home's comfort.

• Install a day/night thermostat in your home so you can better control the temperature. The thermostat will turn your furnace on in the morning before you get up, and it will turn it off whenever you program it to. If you are a working family, you need not keep the heating/cooling on all day. Before you arrive home, the thermostat will turn the heat on so the house will be comfortable when you arrive. Just like magic you can set all your temperature needs with this special thermostat.

• Periodically change your filters in the return air grill. A furnace with a dirty filter will cost more to operate.

Humidifiers

Moist air retains heat. By investing in a humidifier or perhaps adapting your present heating system to include a humidifier, you can lower your thermostat by two to four degrees, which means a savings of four to twelve percent on your total heating bill. In less than five years you will pay for your investment.

Beware of Drippy Water

Do you realize that just one drop of water per second leaking from a faucet can waste 60 gallons of water per week? Washing your hands can use two gallons of hot water. A five-minute shower takes about 20 gallons. And the average dishwasher uses 12–14 gallons of hot water per load. Air-drying the dishes can save up to ten percent of the operating costs.

You may want to check your hot water heater. Did you know that for every 20 degrees the heater dial is lowered, you can cut the energy cost by 25 percent, and if you insulate your heater you can save another 15 percent?

• Take showers instead of baths (believe it or not, showers take less water than baths). A short shower uses four to eight gallons where a bath uses 20 gallons or more.

• If you have a dishwasher, turn it off before the cycle ends and let the dishes air-dry.

• Keep your refrigerator defrosted regularly. Clean those condenser coils on the back and bottom two times a year.

• Keeping your drapes and blinds closed, especially when you're not at home, will keep your home warmer in winter and cooler in summer.

• Fill your swimming pool with rainwater. Attach an elbow connection to your houses' gutter spout and run a pipe from the elbow connection to your pool.

• Prevent sediment from building up in your water heater by draining it periodically.

• Any rooms that are not being used need not be heated, so close the doors and vents (guest rooms, extra baths, closets, etc.). This will help lower heating bills.

• Insulation in the attic is probably the best way to reduce heat loss and air-conditioning loss—a very important and effective way to save on that utility bill!

• Use an insulated blanket for your water heater.

• Use cold water rather than hot water when washing your garments. Many modern fabrics and soaps are actually designed for cold-water washing.

• A moderate temperature setting on your water heater increases an appliance's efficiency since the "normal" setting (usually about 140 degrees F) supplies all the heat most families need.

• If your hot water lines are some distance from your water heater, you may want to wrap them with insulation.

• Add a "water-saver" adapter in each of your shower heads. This will drastically save on water consumption.

Take serious inventory of your energy costs. Particularly when you are on a fixed budget you can acquire added monies for other needs in your home. The area of the country where you live will determine the potential for savings on energy costs in your home.

We all need to be aware of good and dependable stewardship of our natural resources. God intended for us to be good managers of the things He has given us in this world. It makes sense for all of us to conserve and not waste these precious resources.

Waste leads to less money available, and money converts to our hourly labor rate. How much labor do you want to spend or save on utilities?

Chapter 28

Money Management Means Money Saved

"Make all you can, save all you can, give all you can."

JOHN WESLEY

*T*hrift, like fidelity, seems a hopelessly old-fashioned word today. Thrift does and can survive in this day of a throwaway mentality. Thrift signifies a lot more than a simple desire to save for a rainy day or a vacation to Hawaii.

Thrift is a manifestation of a whole complex of still greater virtues—moderation (my Bob's favorite word), reason, self-discipline, maturity—that together make for far more than a mere bank balance. These character words make for a strong and stable life.

Thrift is most of all a sign of character. The kind of life it yields is hard enough to fashion in the best of times. It is much harder to develop in times dominated by the "I-want-it-all-right-now" way of living. We live in a society in which the undisciplined endlessly pursue the unnecessary. Getting something on easy credit is not much of a challenge. Many of us go out and buy more and more and more in order to be satisfied. We don't even have to leave our home. We just tune into a shopping channel or browse through catalogs stuffed with the latest in high-tech gadgets.

Thrifty people save for things, meaning they are less likely to buy a lot of junk. They can face the tease of Madison Avenue and say, "No thank-you."

I have attempted through all of my seminars and books to give my readers some suggestions on how to manage their money. If we would sit down and think as individuals or collectively as families, we could come up with countless ideas to save money. Hopefully, those savings can provide more monies to give unto the Lord. After all, everything belongs to God. He has just loaned it to us for a while. As John Wesley stated,"Make all you can, save all you can, give all you can." What a wonderful formula for managing money! Below I've given you a few starters.

• Decide on some savings goals. One rule of thumb is to save ten percent of pretax income.

• Create a mechanism for saving (e.g., have your bank or credit union automatically transfer a portion of your paycheck into a savings account).

• Record each expenditure you make for one month to determine what discretionary (discretionary dollars are those that can be used to meet long-term goals and objectives) spending can be reduced or eliminated to save more.

• When you budget, be sure to set both short-range and long-range goals. Goals might include a new car next year, a college education for a child ten years from now, and retirement for yourself in 20 years. Setting goals gives you the incentive to control your spending.

• If you are a two-income family, set your standard of living by one of the salaries (usually the husband's, but not always) and live within that income level. Use the other salary to save, invest, or pay cash for larger household items. Don't get caught raising your standard of living to the combined income of both wage earners.

This mistake has led to the undermining of many families.

• Arrange with your creditors so several large household payments don't fall within the same pay period. Stagger the payments throughout the month.

• One simple way to keep expenses down is to pay credit card bills *before* service charges become due. (You must use extreme discipline with credit cards. Not all people can handle the discipline of their proper use. If you can't, go back to a cash-only policy for your purchases.) You can make budgeting easier on yourself if you establish when your regular bills come due each month, including credit card accounts, and work out the most convenient order in which to pay them over the course of the month. If you get organized in this way, you can avoid service charges whenever possible, and you can avoid being hit with a lot of bills that have to be paid at the same time.

• In order to stagger the cost of health care, schedule medical and dental checkups of family members.

• You'll get much more for your shopping dollar if you don't automatically associate brand names and high prices with high-quality merchandise. Some of the best bargains (still high quality) are lower priced or generic.

• You can curtail hospital expenses if you try to avoid being admitted on a Friday. Friday admissions result in longer stays than admission on another day. For the shortest stay, try to have yourself admitted on a Tuesday.

• When you purchase furniture it makes good financial sense to buy the best quality you can afford. Cheap furniture wears out and/or goes out of style quickly. High-quality furniture generally remains in style longer and stays in good condition for many years.

• The best time to buy furniture is in June.

• Cut down on your magazine subscription bills by trading magazines with your neighbors and friends.

• The best time to buy back-to-school clothing for youngsters is at the end of September.

• Money-wise shoppers take advantage of storewide clearance sales after Christmas, Easter, and the Fourth of July. You'll find bargains galore on linens, clothes, china, appliances, and many other items.

• Don't allow yourself to become financially strapped by letting a door-to-door salesperson fast-talk you into signing a sales contract.

• To conserve money, pay cash for things you'll use up soon, such as food items and cleaning supplies. Don't use credit for these items.

• Save gasoline, wear and tear on your car, and time by using mail-order catalogs.

• If you receive a mail-order item after you need it, or it was delayed in shipping and you no longer want the item, just send it back unopened and marked, "refused." Provided the package is unopened, you will not have to pay the return postage.

• When a repair estimate is more than 30 percent of an appliance's cost, seriously consider buying a new appliance.

• To save money on a vacation, look into home-swapping for a stated period of time.

• Don't be afraid to ask for a hotel room's price when you make a reservation. Hotels generally have three room categories: economy, standard, and luxury.

Banking Services

• If you run out of checks and you're standing at a merchant's cash register embarrassed, you can write a check using your deposit slip. Many people aren't aware of this, but your bank will accept this slip and pay. Make sure you complete it as though it were a check. Sign in your normal area of the check.

• Always make it a habit to deposit a check imme-diately after receiving it. This way you minimize your risk of losing the check. I had a lady who came to one of my seminars and got excited about implementing my "Total Mess to Total Rest" program. The next day while cleaning out her desk she found a $200 check that had been in her drawer five months. She immediately called to let me know about her find.

• Ever since I was a young girl I would put my change in a jar. When Bob and I were dating, we would do the same after each date. At the time of our wedding we had almost $400 saved in this manner. Even today I put all of my quarters in a jar. This "pot of gold" has become my "mad" money for a dress, blouse, birthday gift, or such. Many people will faithfully deposit this money in a sav-ings account. It's amazing how this method adds to your savings account.

• Since you want your money working for you, don't keep more than necessary in a no-interest checking account. Even in a business checking account you float extra cash from non-interest to interest to non-interest when it's check-writing time. A few days in the interest account will contribute extra interest over a year's time.

• It usually doesn't pay to postdate a check. If the check is charged to your account earlier than you ex-pected, it might cause other checks that you've written to bounce. This will really cause a loss of your time to straighten out, plus the service charges add up very fast.

• Put your money in a bank account that earns com-pound interest. Your money will work harder for you.

• Only in emergencies should you withdraw funds from a savings account before the stated interest pay-ment date.

• Do all you can to protect your credit rating. This is one of your most valuable assets. If for some reason you run into difficult financial times, go to your creditors *first* and tell them what's happening. If at all possible, they will try to work with you.

• Try to have at least two months of income in your savings account to help during those unannounced emergencies. Six months would be more comfortable if you can manage.

• "Pay yourself first" is a great guideline when deciding to charge or pay cash. If at all possible, pay cash and put the monthly payment into your savings account. That way you get the interest rather than paying the big bad wolf. Over a period of time this will become a normal way of thinking. You can't always do this with large items, but many items can be handled this way.

• Don't pay your bills before they are due. The extra days in an interest-bearing account will give you extra interest each month.

• Banks and savings and loans are not the only institutions for handling money. If you are eligible for membership in a credit union, you would be wise to look at this alternative. Credit unions usually pay higher interest and charge less for loans and credit cards.

• Shop around for the best rates on credit cards. It is a very competitive business and rates do vary. If you are interested in receiving a list comparing over 500 banks, send five dollars to RAM, Box 1700, Frederick, MD 21702 for Card Trak.

• If you must have a credit card, why not get one that will credit your dollar purchases to airplane mileage, hotel accommodations, and even merchandise?

• An idea that pays great dividends is to buy United States saving bonds, either through your local bank or under a payroll savings plan where you're employed.

You can build a sizable nest egg over the years by consistently purchasing a small bond.

• Instead of giving another toy to an "overtoyed" grandchild, purchase a savings bond in the child's name.

• The key to financial success is to spend less than what is earned and continue to do that for a lengthy period of time. Proverbs 13:11 (NIV) says, "He who gathers money little by little makes it grow."

• One of the basic principles of handling your money successfully is to delay gratification. Delayed gratification requires a long-term perspective and is the key to financial maturity. Financial maturity can be defined as "giving up today's desires for future benefits."

• Credit-card companies estimate that using credit cards will result in our spending 34 percent more than if we used cash.

• When confronted with the opportunity to make an impulse purchase, discipline yourself to wait at least one week before spending the money.

• If you are an impulse buyer, ask a spouse or a friend about your purchase before you give yourself the okay to buy the item. With this accountability you will find most of your impulses going away.

• We have some very good friends who freeze all of their credit cards in the freezer. Before they can charge from them, they have to wait until the cards thaw out. In most cases, our friends have changed their minds while they wait.

• If you are really serious about curtailing credit-card spending, place your credit cards (with the exception of one for emergencies) in your safe-deposit box. By the time you go to the trouble of retrieving the cards, you will know if you really need the item and will have had plenty of time to think over the purchase.

Credit Is Like Gold

• A good way to keep out of credit binds is to pay off a series of payments completely before committing yourself to a new series of payments for something else. Also, be cautious of jumping into a home-equity loan. For most families their equity in their home is their retirement savings. If you deplete that fund, you might seriously jeopardize some of your long-term goals.

• If for some reason you get a bad credit rating that has an item improperly posted to your account, you want to correct this error immediately. The longer it remains on your record, the harder it is to get corrected.

• Thinking about taking out a second mortgage to finance a vacation, to buy an automobile, to consolidate bills, or to raise money to buy stocks? Although your home could be used as security for such a loan, it's probably best to take out a personal installment loan instead. Second mortgages should not be used for casual expenditures.

• Try not to put down less than a one-third cash payment when purchasing a car, and don't let the financing extend past 36 months. With less than one-third down, a car's depreciation is likely to reduce its market value faster than you can shrink the balance of the loan.

• Having trouble making monthly loan payments? Consider slicing the remaining payments in half by extending them over a longer period of time.

• Knowing and believing that God owns it all will provide total freedom from any type of financial bondage, whether the bondage of too much or too little. It makes no difference to the person who knows it is all God's.

Insurance Can Be a Saver

• Here's a rule of thumb for how much life insurance you need: the equivalent of four to five years' earnings.

• Avoid having too many policies. Consolidate your program into a few policies rather than buying half a dozen different policies. Your premium will be considerably lower.

• Young couples who usually need more coverage than they can afford should look into a good "term insurance" policy. However, at some time they will want to transfer to a whole life or universal life policy.

• At an early age search out a reputable broker whom you can trust with this very important phase of your financial planning.

• You may be able to save money by paying your premiums annually rather than quarterly or twice a year.

• Today with so many people having video cameras, it would be good to film every room in your home. If not by video, take regular pictures. Store these in a safe-deposit box away from the home. If a claim has to be made, these pictures will show exactly what the property looked like before it was damaged.

• Maintain only the auto insurance coverage you need. You may wish to stop collision and comprehensive coverage on older cars if you can afford to pick up any possible losses yourself. You should, however, have liability insurance on every car you own.

• Tie in your auto insurance with your home insurance. Most companies will give you a good discount if they have your total business. Multiple coverage is a cost savings to you. It also means one less person you have to contact in case of emergencies.

• If you are 65 years of age or older, take advantage of the fact that in many states auto insurance rates are substantially lower for people in this age bracket.

• Take out life insurance policies for your children when they are young. Their future premiums will be reduced because of starting their policies at a younger age than normal.

Be Careful with Home Improvements

• Don't overbuild for your area. When it comes time to sell, you won't be able to get back the value on those improvements.

• Don't invest money in improvements unless you'll get back two dollars for every dollar spent.

• Owners who keep their property for less than three years after making an improvement seldom recover their entire remodeling costs, so plan well ahead when you consider major improvements.

• Check the classified section in your local newspaper to locate someone with good repair skills who will charge you reasonable rates. The best source is through someone who can recommend a worker they have used with satisfaction.

• If you are considering major additions, you might want to look at a neighborhood which has homes that feature these upgrades. By doing your homework you might save a lot of time, money, and stress by buying up.

• It doesn't make sense to remodel an inexpensive home to become an expensive home because the neighborhood will still feature less-expensive homes. If you want a more expensive home, you'll get more for your money in a neighborhood where all the houses are in the high price range.

I trust that these few ideas have given you some thoughts on how you can develop the character trait of "thrift." In 2 Corinthians 9:6 (NASB) Paul said, "He who sows sparingly shall also reap sparingly; and he who sows bountifully shall also reap bountifully." In order for us to sow and reap, we must have something to sow in order to reap. Our surpluses enable us to invest in others' lives. If we are always living on the edge with nothing left, we will never be able to take advantage of God's opportunities for us. "Well done you good and faithful servant. . . . You have been faithful in managing small amounts; so I will put you in charge of large amounts" Matthew 25:21 (Good News Bible). If we are faithful in little things, God will give us larger things to manage. God delegates to us in those areas which we can manage. All things belong to Him. We are given them for just a short period of time. It is so important for us to exercise proper ownership.

Other Good Harvest House Reading

THE 15-MINUTE ORGANIZER
by *Emilie Barnes*

The 15-Minute Organizer is a dream book for the hurried and harried. Its 80 chapters are short and direct so you get right to the answers you need that will let you get ahead and stay ahead when the demands of life threaten to pull you behind.

MORE HOURS IN MY DAY
Updated for the '90s
by *Emilie Barnes*

This time-management, home-organization plan has worked for thousands of people who have attended Emilie's seminars or read her books. Her guidelines, charts, and checklists are the most effective way to get organized—one day at a time. This expanded edition will teach you the secret of finding more hours in your day!

15-MINUTE DEVOTIONS FOR COUPLES
by *Bob* and *Emilie Barnes*

Everything today seems aimed at pulling marriages apart—but it doesn't have to be that way! Fifteen minutes spent together in devotion and prayer each day strengthens a marriage like nothing else. With encouragement and grace, Bob and Emilie share a journey that explores God's majesty and all-sufficient power. Your love for each other and the Lord will increase as you spend this special time together.

THE SPIRIT OF LOVELINESS
by *Emilie Barnes*

Join Emilie Barnes as she shares insights into the inner qualities of spiritual beauty and explores the places of the heart where true femininity is born. With hundreds of "lovely" ideas to help you personalize your home, Emilie shows that beauty *can* be achieved with even the lightest touch of creativity. Your spirit of loveliness will shine through as you make your home a place of prayer, peace, and pleasure for your family.

FILL MY CUP, LORD...
WITH THE PEACE OF YOUR PRESENCE
by *Emilie Barnes*

In short, heartwarming chapters, *Fill My Cup, Lord* comes alive in this honest, uplifting discussion of life's difficult situations. Emilie explores ways to bring joy into any trying circumstance. From trials to triumph, Emilie shares the comfort, thanksgiving, and peace found in our gracious Savior.

THE CREATIVE HOME ORGANIZER
by *Emilie Barnes*

Most of the stress we experience is caused by a lack of organization and can be eliminated with careful planning and timely tips. Bursting with fast and easy methods to save time and energy in your home, *The Creative Home Organizer* has helpful hints for every area of your home. You can learn how to manage a household economically and have fun while doing it! Emilie Barnes also authored *More Hours in My Day* and *Survival for Busy Women*.

15-MINUTE FAMILY TRADITIONS AND MEMORIES
by *Emilie Barnes*

Creating treasured family memories is easier than ever with hundreds of realistic, uncomplicated, and inexpensive ideas from home-management expert Emilie Barnes. Establish new traditions or add spice to favorite family activities with Emilie's simple, unforgettable ideas.

TIME BEGAN IN A GARDEN
by *Emilie Barnes* with *Anne Christian Buchanan*
illustrated by *Glynda Turley*

This exquisitely designed book celebrates the timeless pleasures of God's garden gifts. Filled with quotations, Scripture, and poetry, *Time Began in a Garden* evokes feelings of simplicity, refreshment, and exuberance. A perfect gift for gardeners, people who work with flowers and floral accents, and admirers of fine art, Emilie and Anne share delightful flower lore, decorating ideas, and sweet-smelling sachet recipes—surrounded by the beautiful art of Glynda Turley.

15 MINUTES ALONE WITH GOD
by *Emilie Barnes*

Speaking as someone who has been there, home-management expert Emilie Barnes responds to the cries of women who can't find time for consistent devotions and Bible reading. While helping to develop consistent study habits, Emilie shares from the Bible and her heart meditations of encouragement and direction. The devotions, especially written for busy women, include thoughts on prayer, hospitality, grace, and other subjects close to the heart and home.

IF TEACUPS COULD TALK
by *Emilie Barnes*

Infused with the comforting atmosphere of a gentle afternoon tea, Emilie combines the nostalgic history of English teatime with delightful anecdotes and time-proven recipes. Along with practical helps for a successful teatime, this charmingly illustrated book invites you to enjoy a special time with one friend or several. Sitting over a warm teacup can ease tensions, deepen friendships, and provide an opportunity to open hearts.

THE 15-MINUTE MEAL PLANNER
by *Emilie Barnes* and *Sue Gregg*

Let the *15-Minute Meal Planner* help take the hassle out of meal preparation and introduce your family to a more enjoyable, healthy lifestyle. More than 50 quick-reading chapters provide a wealth of highly practical ideas on food selection, preparation, and storage–along with a helpful starter set of easy and tasty recipes using whole, natural ingredients.

15-MINUTES ALONE WITH GOD FOR MEN
by *Bob Barnes*

Experience the strength, encouragement, and growth that comes from time spent alone with God! In just 15 minutes a day, explore the vast riches and depths of God's power, wisdom, and grace. Each day's devotion includes "Thoughts for Action" which will help you grow closer to God and more effectively love and lead those around you.